T0325626

Free and Open Source Software in Modern Data Science and Business Intelligence:

Emerging Research and Opportunities

K.G. Srinivasa
CBP Government Engineering College, India

Ganesh Chandra Deka
M. S. Ramaiah Institute of Technology, India

Krishnaraj P.M.
M. S. Ramaiah Institute of Technology, India

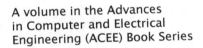
A volume in the Advances
in Computer and Electrical
Engineering (ACEE) Book Series

IGI Global
DISSEMINATOR OF KNOWLEDGE

Published in the United States of America by
IGI Global
Engineering Science Reference (an imprint of IGI Global)
701 E. Chocolate Avenue
Hershey PA, USA 17033
Tel: 717-533-8845
Fax: 717-533-8661
E-mail: cust@igi-global.com
Web site: http://www.igi-global.com

Library of Congress Cataloging-in-Publication Data

Names: Srinivasa, K. G., author. | Deka, Ganesh Chandra, 1969- author. | M.,
   Krishnaraj P., 1980- author.
Title: Free and open source software in modern data science and business
   intelligence : emerging research and opportunities / by K.G. Srinivasa,
   Ganesh Chandra Deka, and Krishnaraj P.M.
Description: Hershey, PA : Engineering Science Reference, [2018] | Includes
   bibliographical references.
Identifiers: LCCN 2017020858| ISBN 9781522537076 (hardcover) | ISBN
   9781522537083 (ebook)
Subjects: LCSH: Open source software.
Classification: LCC QA76.76.O62 S74 2018 | DDC 005.3--dc23 LC record available at https://lccn.
loc.gov/2017020858

This book is published in the IGI Global book series Advances in Computer and Electrical
Engineering (ACEE) (ISSN: 2327-039X; eISSN: 2327-0403)

British Cataloguing in Publication Data
A Cataloguing in Publication record for this book is available from the British Library.

All work contributed to this book is new, previously-unpublished material.
The views expressed in this book are those of the authors, but not necessarily of the publisher.

For electronic access to this publication, please contact: eresources@igi-global.com.

Advances in Computer and Electrical Engineering (ACEE) Book Series

ISSN:2327-039X
EISSN:2327-0403

Editor-in-Chief: Srikanta Patnaik, SOA University, India

MISSION

The fields of computer engineering and electrical engineering encompass a broad range of interdisciplinary topics allowing for expansive research developments across multiple fields. Research in these areas continues to develop and become increasingly important as computer and electrical systems have become an integral part of everyday life.

The **Advances in Computer and Electrical Engineering (ACEE) Book Series** aims to publish research on diverse topics pertaining to computer engineering and electrical engineering. **ACEE** encourages scholarly discourse on the latest applications, tools, and methodologies being implemented in the field for the design and development of computer and electrical systems.

COVERAGE

- Programming
- Computer Hardware
- Analog Electronics
- Algorithms
- Circuit Analysis
- Sensor Technologies
- Applied Electromagnetics
- Optical Electronics
- Digital Electronics
- Computer science

IGI Global is currently accepting manuscripts for publication within this series. To submit a proposal for a volume in this series, please contact our Acquisition Editors at Acquisitions@igi-global.com or visit: http://www.igi-global.com/publish/.

Titles in this Series

For a list of additional titles in this series, please visit:
https://www.igi-global.com/book-series/advances-computer-electrical-engineering/73675

Design and Use of Virtualization Technology in Cloud Computing
Prashanta Kumar Das (Government Industrial Training Institute Dhansiri, India) and Ganesh
Chandra Deka (Government of Indi, India)
Engineering Science Reference • ©2018 • 315pp • H/C (ISBN: 9781522527855) • US $235.00

Smart Grid Test Bed Using OPNET and Power Line Comunication
Jun-Ho Huh (Catholic University of Pusan, South Korea)
Engineering Science Reference • ©2018 • 425pp • H/C (ISBN: 9781522527763) • US $225.00

Transport of Information-Carriers in Semiconductors and Nanodevices
Muhammad El-Saba (Ain-Shams University, Egypt)
Engineering Science Reference • ©2017 • 677pp • H/C (ISBN: 9781522523123) • US $225.00

Accelerating the Discovery of New Dielectric Properties in Polymer Insulation
Boxue Du (Tianjin University, China)
Engineering Science Reference • ©2017 • 388pp • H/C (ISBN: 9781522523093) • US $210.00

Handbook of Research on Nanoelectronic Sensor Modeling and Applications
Mohammad Taghi Ahmadi (Urmia University, Iran) Razali Ismail (Universiti Teknologi
Malaysia, Malaysia) and Sohail Anwar (Penn State University, USA)
Engineering Science Reference • ©2017 • 579pp • H/C (ISBN: 9781522507369) • US $245.00

Field-Programmable Gate Array (FPGA) Technologies for High Performance Instrumentation
Julio Daniel Dondo Gazzano (University of Castilla-La Mancha, Spain) Maria Liz Crespo
(International Centre for Theoretical Physics, Italy) Andres Cicuttin (International Centre for
Theoretical Physics, Italy) and Fernando Rincon Calle (University of Castilla-La Mancha,
Spain)
Engineering Science Reference • ©2016 • 306pp • H/C (ISBN: 9781522502999) • US $185.00

For an enitre list of titles in this series, please visit:
https://www.igi-global.com/book-series/advances-computer-electrical-engineering/73675

701 East Chocolate Avenue, Hershey, PA 17033, USA
Tel: 717-533-8845 x100 • Fax: 717-533-8661
E-Mail: cust@igi-global.com • www.igi-global.com

Table of Contents

Preface..vii

Chapter 1
An Exploratory Analysis and Classification of Papers Presented in a Decade
of OSS Conferences Using Revised Taxonomy.......................................1

Chapter 2
Macro Studies of FOSS Ecology 58

Chapter 3
Micro Studies of FOSS Ecology..67

Chapter 4
Studies of Project Tasks 81

Chapter 5
Exploratory Analysis of Free and Open Source Software Ecology.......93

Chapter 6
Finding Influential Nodes in Sourceforge.net Using Social Network
Analysis...104

Chapter 7
Graph Mining Approaches to Study Volunteer Relationships in Sourceforge.
net..117

Chapter 8
A Multi-Step Process Towards Integrating Free and Open Source Software in
Engineering Education...140

Conclusion 151

Appendix... 156

Related Readings.. 168

Index.. 189

Preface

Free and Open Source Software (FOSS) consists of two sub-cultures, namely, Free Software and Open Source Software, within the same movement. Though both subscribe to same philosophy they differ in their relationship with proprietary software (software which is released without source code). Free Software insists on ethical and moral importance of users' freedom and hence has strict norms on how to bundle free and proprietary software together. Open Source Software has a pragmatic view on this matter and allows proprietary software to be easily bundled with open source software. So both Free Software and Open Source Software has a separate set of licenses, which govern the distribution terms of software according to their terms. In this work, the unified term FOSS is used to refer to both camps unless specified otherwise.

FOSS refers both to the unique development model and innovative distribution policy of software. The ecology of FOSS comprises of people, organizations and software. People having expertise in software development activities like analysis, design, coding, testing and translation is its main actors. Numbering more than 800,000 (Crowston, Wei, Howison et al., 2012), they are globally distributed (Simmons & Dillon, 2006, Oezbek, 2010), motivated and restless (Rossi, Russo & Succi, 2009). Common users, researchers and curious bystanders are also part of this narrative. Universities, government and non-government organizations and increasingly many private firms are becoming part of FOSS ecology (Crowston, Wei, Howison et al., 2012). The creation, distribution and consumption of software are the main activity here. FOSS is healthy software ecology, where thousands of different software interacts among them to satisfy the user requirements (German & Gonzalez-Barahona, 2009). There are philosophies and beliefs, rituals and policies, prophets and heroes whose familiarity is the key to understand this phenomenon. That the process of developing software and the software product, thus created both are available for public scrutiny and consumption is its major uniqueness.

FOSS has attracted the attention of people from diverse backgrounds who have labelled it as an opportunistic software development model (Umarji, Sim & Lopes, 2008), alternative development model for software, new economic and marketing premise (Gonzalez-Barahona, Martınez, Polo et al., 2008), software licensing philosophy (Lyn, 2009), movement (Kuechler, Jensen & Bryant, 2013), social and economic phenomenon (Krogh, Haefliger, Spaeth et al., 2012). The utopian idea of FOSS is well captured by an author (Kelty, 2008). This almost religious explanation is most common among many writers (Noll, 2009).

Today FOSS is in ascending with the total number of open source software projects and the total amount of open source code in the world, are growing at an exponential rate. The total amount of source code and the total number of projects double about every 14 months (Deshpande & Riehle, 2008). But its beginnings were very humble. The evolution of FOSS can be traced in three stages: Free Software period (1980's), Open Source period (1998 onwards) and Growth period (2000 onwards) where government policies and business adoption fuelled its growth (Jensen C., Scacchi W., 2011). The roots of FOSS are in the practices of hackers during the 1970s (DAndrea, DePaoli & Teli, 2008). As Stephen Levvys notes in his book 'Hackers: heroes of computer revolution' (Levy, 2001) the early hackers influenced by counterculture movements of those times shaped most of the core technologies and beliefs which are still followed. The main aspect of FOSS, which is the unrestricted sharing of software along with the source code, was the mainstay of hacker culture (McKenzie, 2004). With computers being used only by large corporations and public institutions, university departments (MIT AI Lab), student groups (Tech Model Railroad Club), hobbyist networks (Homebrew Computer Club) were the breeding grounds for new ideas and software.

The introduction of computer kits (Altair 8800) and personal computers (IBM PC) in late 1970's and early 1980s changed the landscape of software. With a commercial value of software being understood by companies, they began to question the free sharing philosophy (Gates B., 1976). The university departments too began to use software produced by companies who refused to share the source code, as it was the practice till then. It is during this period, Richard M Stallman (RMS) took the first step towards institutionalizing Free Software. His crusade started with the conflicts between the institutional goals and the virtues of individuals valued by the social practice. The restriction to access the source code was considered wrong by RMS as it would hinder "… humanity's rapidly growing need for better and better technologies." (Krogh, Haefliger, Spaeth et al., 2012). His contribution ranges from defining Free

Software, starting an institution Free Software Foundation (FSF) to protect the interest of free software, a project which aimed at creating an entire free operation system GNUs Not Unix (GNU), and a legal mechanism to distribute free software GNU General Public License (GPL).

Free Software does not refer to the price of software, but to the liberty users get by using it (Stallman, 1999). The freedoms guaranteed by Free Software are to Run, Modify, Redistribute original and modified versions of software. Access to source code is necessary to make these freedoms effective. To enable these freedoms and to ensure companies do not change the terms of distribution, RMS used the concept of copyright in an intelligent manner. Copyrights are used to:

1. Assert the ownership of a work.
2. To determine the distribution terms of the work.

Normally copyright holders restrict the distribution of their works, but RMS used the same law to ensure that the copyrighted work will remain in public domain forever. To enable this, he defined the term Copyleft that is wordplay on Copyright. Copyleft insists that one register the copyright of his work to assert the ownership but does not restrict the access to work as usually done. Instead copyleft allows unrestricted usage, distribution and modification of the work. The GNU General Public License (GPL) was the first license and still a popular one, which embodies this spirit of software commons.

The role of RMS in Free Software is not limited to an armchair philosopher. He is a hacker par-excellence and has contributed a lot of tools, which are widely used even today. The legendary editors, Emacs, the GNU Complier Collection (GCC), and GNU Debugger (GDB) are all proofs for his talents as a hacker. These tools were developed as part of larger project GNU (recursive acronym for GNUs Not Unix), which aimed at creating a complete Unix-like operating system with complete Free Software components (Stallman et al., 1985). It was during this process that the distributed software development involving various interested developers was practised. The contribution of Free Software sub-culture of FOSS therefore is manifold. It laid philosophical, legal, social and technical foundation for the emergence of next important player in this story.

Even if all other components were ready, kernel was missing from the proposed complete free operating system. In the other part of world, a Finnish student Linus Torvalds initiated a project to develop an operating system titled Linux using major tools from GNU project. The Linux project too involved public participation and its success signalled the arrival of complete operating system, which should be rightly called GNU-Linux. The GNU-Linux soon became popular and the public development method it used became a reference model for many other projects. Some participants in this wave also started to document their experience and formulated theories explaining why this method works. One such document 'The Cathedral and the Bazaar' (Raymond, 2001) evoked much attention and famously the Mozilla project used these practices to regain its sliding market share in browser market.

With the emergence of the Internet, it was possible for people outside the university, research institutes and public organizations to participate in the new software development movement. Also, Internet was fuelled by host of Free Software tools like sendmail and BIND. With the dot-com bubble starting to emerge, the stage was set for business to embrace Free Software in a big way. FOSS is not anti-commercial but there are attempts to paint it as one (Ljungberg, 2000). Skeptics started arguing that Free in Free Software does not send right signal to the business world and there is a need to reform the movement to make it more market friendly. This led to the emergence of Open Source as a marketing term for Free Software. But Open Source was much more than that. It silently diluted the ethical principles of Free Software and made it easier for corporates and individuals who wanted to commercialize Free Software and restrict its distribution terms.

As RMS brilliantly put it, Open Source is just a development option but Free Software is a philosophy. Open Source as a means of creating good software views the public development methodology but for Free Software it is an end in itself (Ljungberg, 2000). Free Software cares for the freedom of users and has enough legal safeguards to stop anyone from appropriating the work of many volunteers who contribute to the software. Free Software allows non-Free Software to be combined with Free Software provided the source code of non-Free Software also be distributed along. Free Software licenses also do not allow anyone to change the distribution terms attached by its original author. In contrast, Open Source in the guise of making software licence not distinguish between products allows mixing of non-Free Software without any restrictions and change the distribution terms. By the end of last millennium FOSS had established itself as a credible alternative to proprietary software. Today it has captured public imagination, attracted governments and large private firms, developed huge body of research and FOSS are an important part of modern software infrastructure.

In summary, the Free and Open Source phenomena is the result of distributed collaboration among volunteers across the globe, which was aided and shaped by the following historical factors

- **Hardware:** Growth of personal computers.
- **Network:** Proliferation of Internet.
- **Software:** UNIX, communication and collaboration tools, software development tools.
- **People:** Trained and/or self-educated geeks.
- **Culture:** Commons, liberty, and individuality.
- **Law:** Copyright, software licenses, monopoly law (which forced AT&T to downplay the impact of UNIX).

MOTIVATION

Eric Raymond said in his classic work 'The Cathedral and the Bazaar' that 'personal itch' motivates a person to take up a software project. Similarly, a strong personal reason motivated this researcher to take up the current work. After using, evangelising and believing in the philosophy of FOSS it was natural that this researcher selected to study the development model of FOSS. FOSS presents a utopian dream where a global network of selfless programmers create software of quality and yet give it away for no fees and also liberally permit its modification and redistribution by giving away the source code. The success of project like GNU-Linux makes the premise much more appealing. Also, the early reports by participants suggest that traditional software engineering practices are not followed in FOSS development. Therefore, it became necessary for this researcher to undertake a detailed study of this domain. Also, it was necessary to interpret the phenomenon in a better way and convince others to join the movement. Hence this researcher has taken up this work to satisfy his own doubts and questions regarding the working, valid and longevity of FOSS more than anything else.

But understanding the phenomenon of FOSS becomes important for other reasons also. There is a growing interest regarding FOSS among governments, corporates, educational institutes and general public. IT infrastructure of any organisation today inevitably has at least some FOSS components. While many are attracted to FOSS because of it low or no licence fees, the possibility of changing and extending the software is an added advantage. In developing countries FOSS can be a way to bring the power of computers to the common people. Freedom from vendor lock-ins is another key factor for FOSS adoption. But the promise of freedoms to use, modify and redistribute the software in ones own terms makes FOSS unique. In the view of increased appeal and usage of FOSS, it is necessary to understand FOSS phenomenon more deeply.

The public participation model of FOSS development appears to be an experiment in failure in the beginning. That a set of uncoordinated developers without formal governance structure and control mechanisms, communicating almost exclusively through Internet to develop working software is a challenge to the traditional software engineering theories. Initial observers too applied visual metaphors like Bazaar to explain this phenomenon, which further cemented the chaotic notion regarding FOSS development. Therefore, it is necessary to study the development practices followed in FOSS to examine its uniqueness so that it can be replicated in other projects. To do this the available literature in the field should be critically reviewed. Then experiments regarding the developer collaborations have to be conducted. And finally, as this researcher is involved in education sector, it is also important to learn how the benefits of FOSS can be brought into classrooms.

More specifically the questions attempted in this work are as follows:

1. What is the current state of research in FOSS?
2. Is FOSS ecology evolving to support the modern IT needs?
3. What are the approaches that can be followed to understand developer relations in FOSS?
4. How can FOSS be applied effectively in engineering education?

ORGANIZATION OF THE BOOK

Chapter 1 summarizes the research done in the domain of FOSS. During the literature review, it was found that the existing taxonomies used for FOSS research could be improved to better reflect the changes in the field. Therefore, an existing taxonomy was revised and all the 347 papers presented in Open Source Systems (OSS) conferences from 2005 2014 were mapped to this taxonomy. This chapter discusses the important works in various areas like developer motivation, volunteer participation, community growth, software development practices and quality assurance models in FOSS. This chapter also provides an overview of research efforts in FOSS and its challenges.

Chapter 2 deals with the macro studies of FOSS ecology. The focus of this chapter is to find the general trends among the large numbers of projects found in the repository of FOSS projects, namely, Sourceforge.net. The features such as number of projects, number of developers working in FOSS projects are analysed. The data from Feb 2005 to Aug 2009 are considered for the study. This chapter also covers the issue of single developer projects in FOSS.

The focus of Chapter 3 is the study of successful projects in FOSS ecology. Six projects between the two-lakh projects are selected for a detailed study. The numbers of developers working on these projects, the nature of their contribution and the movement pattern of developers across multiple projects within FOSS ecology are covered.

The study of tasks involved in the projects is the focus of Chapter 4. The number of tasks in each project, time taken for completing the tasks, the allocation of tasks to developers and the amount of tasks they complete are discussed here.

Chapter 5 describes the ecology of FOSS through a popular repository Sourceforge.net which hosts more than 300,000 projects. The evolution of developers and projects from 2005 to 2013 are studied. The developer relations are mapped as a social network and analysed. The existence of power law in Sourceforge.net is verified. Rubyforge and Freecode, which are becoming important repositories, are also studied for developer relations.

Chapter 6 focuses on finding influential nodes in Sourceforge.net by using Social Network Analysis approaches. High Degree, LDAG, SPS-CELF++ and SimPath algorithms are used on the same dataset to discover most influential developers. The computational resources used by these algorithms are also studied. The consistency of top developers across multiple years are also analysed to understand the longevity of good developers.

Chapter 7 applies Graph Mining techniques to Sourceforge.net to understand the developer relationships. First the top developers are discovered using a popular algorithm Pagerank. Based on the existing links between the developers, their future collaborations are predicted using Link Prediction algorithm. The accuracy of the results is verified using the measures of precision and recall. Frequent subgraphs are mined using gSpan and SUBDUE algorithms. K spanning and Highly Connected Subgraphs clustering techniques are used to find cliques of developers.

Chapter 8 outlines a three-stage process, which can be applied to adopt FOSS in engineering education. First the advantages and need for using FOSS in classrooms is discussed. Later the first step FOSS Introduction where teachers should also sensitise students regarding the history and philosophy of FOSS is outlined. In FOSS Diffusion stage teachers are required to use FOSS artefacts beyond software in courses. Offering the separate course in FOSS is required in FOSS Adoption stage. The outline of the course offered by this researcher is listed for reference purposes.

Lastly, the Conclusion summaries the major findings reported in this work.

REFERENCES

Cerbo, F. D., Dodero, G., & Succi, G. (2008). Social networking technologies for free-open source e-learning systems. In Open Source Development, Communities and Quality (pp. 289–297). Springer.

Crowston, K., Wei, K., Howison, J., & Wiggins, A. (2012). Free/libre open-source software development: What we know and what we do not know. *ACM Computing Surveys*, *44*(2).

DAndrea, V., DePaoli, S., & Teli, M. (2008). Open to grok. how do hacker's practices produce hackers? In Open Source Development, Communities and Quality (pp. 121–129). Springer.

Deshpande, A., & Riehle, D. (2008) The total growth of open source. In Open Source Development, Communities and Quality (pp. 197–209). Springer. doi:10.1007/978-0-387-09684-1_16

Gates B. (1976). *An open letter to hobbyists*. Academic Press.

German, D. M., & Gonza'lez-Barahona, J. M. (2009). An empirical study of the reuse of software licensed under the gnu general public license. In Open Source Ecosystems: Diverse Communities Interacting (pp. 185–198). Springer. doi:10.1007/978-3-642-02032-2_17

Gonzalez-Barahona, M. J., Martınez, A., Polo, A., Hierro J.J., Reyes, M., Soriano, J., & Fernandez, R. (2008). The networked forge: new environments for libre software development. In Open Source Development, Communities and Quality (pp. 299–306). Springer.

Howison, J., Conklin, M., & Ossmole, K. C. (2005). A collaborative repository for floss research data and analyses. In *Proceedings of the First International Conference on Open Source Systems*, Genova.

Jensen, C., & Scacchi, W. (2011). License update and migration processes in open source software projects. In Open Source Systems: Grounding Research (pp. 177–195). Springer.

Kelty, C. M. (2008). Two bits: The cultural significance of free software. Duke University Press.

Krogh, G. V., Haefliger, S., Spaeth, S., & Wallin, M. W. (2012). Carrots and rainbows: Motivation and social practice in open source software development. *Management Information Systems Quarterly*, *36*(2), 649–676.

Kuechler, V., Jensen, C., & Bryant, D. (2013). Misconceptions and barriers to adoption of foss in the us energy industry. In Open Source Software: Quality Verification (pp. 232–244). Springer.

Levy S., (2001). *Hackers: Heroes of the computer revolution* (vol. 4). Penguin Books.

Ljungberg, J. (2000). Open source movements as a model for organising. *European Journal of Information Systems*, *9*(4), 208–216. doi:10.1057/palgrave.ejis.3000373

Lyn, P. C. (2009). A survey of usability practices in free/libre/open source software. In Open Source Ecosystems: Diverse Communities Interacting (pp. 264–273). Springer.

McKenzie, W. (2004). *A hacker manifesto*. Academic Press.

Noll, J. (2009). What constitutes open source? a study of the vista electronic medical record software. In Open Source Ecosystems: Diverse Communities Interacting (pp. 310–319). Springer.

Oezbek, C. (2010). Introducing automated unit testing into open source projects. In Open Source Software: New Horizons (pp. 361–366). Springer. doi:10.1007/978-3-642-13244-5_32

Raymond, E. S. (2001). The Cathedral & the Bazaar: Musings on linux and open source by an accidental revolutionary. O'Reilly Media, Inc.

Rossi, B., Russo, B., & Succi, G. (2009). Analysis of open source software development iterations by means of burst detection techniques. In Open Source Ecosystems: Diverse Communities Interacting (pp. 83–93). Springer. doi:10.1007/978-3-642-02032-2_9

Simmons, G. L., & Dillon, T. S. (2006). Towards an ontology for open source software development. In *Open Source Systems* (pp. 65–75). Springer. doi:10.1007/0-387-34226-5_7

Stallman, R. (1985). *The GNU manifesto*. Academic Press.

Stallman R. (1999). The gnu operating system and the free software movement. In *Open sources: Voices from the open source revolution* (Vol. 1, p. 280). Academic Press.

Umarji, M., Sim, E. S., & Lopes, C. (2008). Archetypal internetscale source code searching. In *Open source development, communities and quality* (pp. 257–263). Springer. doi:10.1007/978-0-387-09684-1_21

Chapter 1

An Exploratory Analysis and Classification of Papers Presented in a Decade of OSS Conferences Using Revised Taxonomy

ABSTRACT

On the occasion of completion of ten years of Open Source Systems (OSS) conferences, this paper studies its contribution to the extension of Free and Open Source Software (FOSS) research. An existing taxonomy was used to initially classify the 347 full and short papers presented in the conferences. Because there were many new categories, which did not fit, in existing system, the taxonomy was revised and the reclassified papers are presented in this paper. The analysis of locations, themes, participants and citations of successive conferences results in interesting observation. The major takeaway of this ongoing study is to demonstrate that the goal of OSS conferences, as mentioned in the first edition, "to promote the exchange of new ideas, research and applications in the emerging field of Open Source Software," is more than successful.

DOI: 10.4018/978-1-5225-3707-6.ch001

INTRODUCTION

Though Free and Open Source Software (FOSS) is used together throughout the discussion of this work, it is necessary to understand that there are certain differences between the two. The differences, though minor in appearance have deep philosophical implications on the way software is discussed. Therefore, it is necessary to understand the definition of both terms.

Free software is a matter of the users' freedom to run, copy, distribute, study, change and improve the software. More precisely, it means that the program's users have the four essential freedoms:

1. The freedom to run the program, for any purpose (freedom 0).
2. The freedom to study how the program works, and change it to make it do what you wish (freedom 1). Access to the source code is a precondition for this.
3. The freedom to redistribute copies so you can help your neighbor (freedom 2).
4. The freedom to improve the program, and release your improvements (and modified versions in general) to the public, so that the whole community benefits (freedom 3). Access to the source code is a precondition for this.

In 1998, a group of individuals advocated that the term free software should be replaced by open source software(OSS) as an expression, which is less ambiguous and more comfortable for the corporate world. The open source label came out of a strategy session held in Palo Alto in reaction to Netscape's January 1998 announcement of a source code release for Navigator (as Mozilla). Eric S. Raymond and Bruce Perens formed the Open Source Initiative (OSI) in February 1998.

The definition of 'Open Source Software' as maintained by OSI is as follows.

Open source doesn't just mean access to the source code. The distribution terms of open-source software must comply with the following criteria:

1. **Free Redistribution:** The license shall not restrict any party from selling or giving away the software as a component of an aggregate software distribution containing programs from several different sources. The license shall not require a royalty or other fee for such sale.

2. **Source Code:** The program must include source code, and must allow distribution in source code as well as compiled form. Where some form of a product is not distributed with source code, there must be a well-publicized means of obtaining the source code for no more than a reasonable reproduction cost preferably, downloading via the Internet without charge. The source code must be the preferred form in which a programmer would modify the program. Deliberately obfuscated source code is not allowed. Intermediate forms such as the output of a preprocessor or translator are notallowed.

3. **Derived Works:** The license must allow modifications and derived works, and must allow them to be distributed under the same terms as the license of the originalsoftware.

4. **Integrity of The Author's Source Code:** The license may restrict source-code from being distributed in modified form only if the license allows the distribution of "patch files" with the source code for the purpose of modifying the program at build time. The license must explicitly permit distribution of software built from modified source code. The license mayrequirederived works to carry a different name or version number from the original software.

5. **No Discrimination Against Persons or Groups:** The license must not discriminate against any person or group of persons.

6. **No Discrimination Against Fields of Endeavor:** The license must not restrict any one from making use of the program in a specific field of endeavor. For example, it may not restrict the program from being used in a business, or from being used for genetic research.

7. **Distribution of License:** The rights attached to the program must apply to all to whom the program is redistributed without the need for execution of an additional license by those parties.

8. **License Must Not Be Specific to a Product:** The rights attached to the program must not depend on the program's being part of a particular soft-ware distribution. If the program is extracted from that distribution and used or distributed within the terms of the program's license, all parties to whom the program is redistributed should have the same rights as those that are granted in conjunction with the original software distribution.

9. **License Must Not Restrict Other Software:** The license must not place restrictions on other software that is distributed along with the licensed software. For example, the license must not insist that all other programs distributed on the same medium must be open-source software.

10. **License Must Be Technology-Neutral:** No provision of the license may be predicated on any individual technology or style of interface.

The essential difference between free software and open source software is in the way they treat the software licenses. While most free software licenses are viral i.e the derived works also must be released using the same license as the source work, the open source licences do not impose these restrictions. Apart from this, there is a general complaint against open source camp that they do not emphasize on the essential quality of freedom, which is the central theme offree software. But the open source proponents claim that the use of free makes the whole issue looks unattractive for commercial players and hence they use the term opensoftware.

The important feature of free and open source software has been the invitation to interested programmers to join the development work. In his 'The GNU Manifesto' Richard Stallman mentioned his intentions clearly when he said, "I am asking individuals for donations of programs and work." From the begining volunteers have contributed immensely to the success of this movement. Continuing this trend, Linus Trovalds appealed to the computer users to give him suggestions regarding his implementation in 1991. He said, "I would like to know what features most people would want. Any suggestions are welcome, but I won't promise I will implement them".

The success of FOSS is often attributed to this phenomenon of involving volunteers in the development process. The virtual absence of any restriction to join any project is in direct contrast to the established practices of development in the proprietary software. The expanding Internet and the improvements in the communication and project management technologies help the global nature of development model. By their open nature of development FOSS has left many open questions some of which this book intends to answer.

Because of its complex nature involving multiple actors like volunteers, paid developers, firms, technology and culture FOSS has eluded a singular interpretation. Researchers have been trying to understand the phenomenon of FOSS in many different ways. It was Eric Raymond who famously invoked the visual metaphor of 'Cathedral and Bazaar' to explain FOSS. In his original formulation the development of free soft ware products like emacs followed the cathedral model with only authorized developers able to participate in the process. In contrast Linus followed a more open, public form of development involving any interested developer, which he labeled as 'Bazaar'. Over the years while 'Bazaar' has expanded to include both the free software and open software development models, 'Cathedral' has come to sign if proprietary and commercial software development models.

Richard Stallman had argued that the digital properties of software (e.g., easy copying and distribution) make it possible to treat it as a public rather than a private good, and as a result, users of software should be provided the freedom to use, distribute, and modify the software in any way they might desire. Charles Schweik carried forward this idea and applied the Institutional Analysis and Development (IAD) Framework of Elinor Ostrom to interpret FOSS as a form of 'software commons' (Hess & Ostrom, 2005). Unlike in other commons, the challenge in FOSS commons is how to achieve collective action to create and maintain a commons or public good rather than the issue of protecting an existing commons from destruction.

(Schweik, 2007) found that the key to the success of FOSS common-property regimes was the willingness of a programmer to contribute to the collaborative effort (the action in the Framework), and the cumulative efforts of at least small teams of actors to collectively produce and maintain software (an outcome). Such regime depends on:

1. The design and structure of rules in use,
2. The human community participating in FOSS, and
3. The physical or material environment.

More elaborately the necessary conditions for success of FOSS as commons are

1. Motivated development team who should sustain the project for consider- able point of time and hand it over to capable parties when it gets disinterested
2. Modularised software design so that individuals can contribute
3. Tool support to contribute and manage distributed development and communication tools to collaborate
4. Organisational rules, hierarchical decision making, scope for growth within the community and appropriate reward/punishment processes.

FOSS is interpreted also as gift economy which is based on the principle of reciprocity, upholds the idea of software as a public good as compared to proprietary software as exchange economy which relies predominantly on monetary flows, market transactions and is organised around a scarcity of resources (Berdou & Dini, 2005). FOSS is also understood as a form of

E.Wenger's 'communities of practice'. FOSS developers often self-organize into organizational forms that are characterized as evolving socio-technical interaction networks (STINs) (Scacchi, 2005). Recently there has been an attempt to label the practices in FOSS as 'Citizen Engineering' (Zhai, Kijewski-Correa, Kareem, Hachen & Madey, 2012).

The Influence and Reach of FOSS

Benkler explains the phenomenon of FOSS through the model of Commons based peer production (CBPP) (Benkler & Nissenbaum, 2006). CBPP takes place in the ubiquitous digital networks and the wide distribution of low cost physical capital, results in a conducive situation for creativity and mass participation. Three factors are considered as important for the success of CBPD, which are all exhibited by FOSS-components, should be modular, majority of modules should be smaller and integration cost of modules should be low. This model of global volunteer collaboration and transparent process has influenced Open Access, Open Data, Free Culture and Open Hardware (Viseur, 2012). It has made states adopt Open Governance (Lakka, Stamati & Martakos, 2012). Open Reference Models (Koch, Strecker & Frank, 2006), Open Innovation (Kilamo, Hammouda, Kairamo, Rasanen & Saarinen, 2012) and Open Content exemplified by Wikipedia are extensions of FOSS principles (Pfaff & Hasan, 2007; Anthony, Smith & Williamson, 2005).

FOSS methods and software are employed in One Laptop Per Child project (Garbett, Lieser & Boldyreff, 2010). They are used to provide solutions for visually impaired people (Boccacci, Carrega & Dodero, 2007). The process followed in FOSS development are being used to find cure to tropical diseases, develop Health Information Systems Programme (Staring & Titlestad, 2006), build occupational health application (Tiangco, Stockwell, Sapsford, Rainer & Swanton, 2005), transform casebooks in law (Bodie, 2005), manage air traffic (Hardy & Bourgois, 2006), automate agricultural irrigation system (Jaime & Fernandez, 2014) and even change the dynamics of gaming industry (Scacchi, 2011).

It is argued that the commercial form of FOSS is emerging as OSS 2.0 (Fitzgerald, 2006). This is clear by looking at the adoption of FOSS across countries and organizations. It is reported that 87% of US businesses use FLOSS (Crowston, Wei, Howison & Wiggins, 2012). European Union too is embracing FOSS with specific information available from Norway (Hauge & Ziemer, 2009), Germany (Dobusch, 2008), Swedan (Lundell,

Lings & Lindqvist, 2006) (Lundell & Lings, 2010), Italy (Davini, Faggioni & Tartari, 2005) (Banzi, Bruno & Caire, 2008; Lorenzi & Rossi, 2008), Netherlands(Ravesteyn & Silvius, 2008) and Belgium (Ven, Nuffel & Verelst, 2006; Ven & Verelst, 2006). To appreciate its global reach, one can study the usage and impact of FOSS in Brazil (Pinto & Kamei, 2014), Cuba (Gon, Boodraj & Cabreja, 2014), Japan (Noda & Tansho, 2010; Noda, Tansho & Coughlan, 2013; Noda & Tansho, 2014), Africa (Brink, Roos, Weller, & Van Belle, 2006; Sowe & McNaughton, 2012) and India (Henttonen, 2011). Large companies like Hewlett-Packard (Melian & Mahring, 2008) and Nokia (Jaaksi, 2007) (Lindman, Rossi, Marttiin, 2008) too are reported to be adopting FOSS practices.

Research in FOSS and Its Challenges

FOSS has moved from an academic curiosity to a mainstream focus for research (Crowston, Wei, Howison & Wiggins, 2012). Because of its complex nature involving multiple actors like volunteers, paid developers, firms, technology and culture FOSS has eluded a singular interpretation. Researchers have been trying to understand the phenomenon of FOSS in many different ways. Researchers study FOSS projects in order to better understand collaborative human behavior during the process of building software (Howison, Conklin, & Ossmole, 2005). Like archaeologists, empirical software engineering researchers often seek to understand people. The FOSS movement is particularly important to software engineering research, since project artifacts, such as source code, revision control histories, and message boards, are openly available to softwarearchaeologists (Pratt, MacLean, Knutson & Ringger, 2011). But undertaking research in FOSS is not easy. Whereas data analysis about proprietary software practices was primarily a problem of scarcity (getting access and permissions to use the data), collecting and analyzing FOSS data becomes a problem of abundance and reliability (storage, sharing, aggregation, and filtering of the data) (Conklin, 2006). Initial attempts in this area focused on asking questions about developer participation. With much data available, a researcher remarked it is difficult to get preliminary details of FOSS projects (Conklin, 2006). From the initial days of bewilderment, FOSS research has grown in strength during the last decade.

Availability of real, large and reliable data is critical to any research. Due to its promise of developing software in public, there is an avalanche of data generated by FOSS projects. Not only the technical artefacts like cvs records, source code, bug reports and patches but the communication trails like emails, chat transcripts and tweets are also available for researchers to reconstruct the entire sequence of events leading to the final release of software. While most popular products have their own websites many projects are hosted in places like sourceforge, github, freashmeat, who provide the common facilities required starting and sustaining a FOSS project. These repositories have become happy hunting ground for researchers looking for real data (Koch, 2005; Dawid, et al., 2005; Rainer, Stephen, 2005; Sowe, Angelis, Stamelos & Manolopoulos, 2007). With the start of FLOSSmole project (Howison, Conklin & Ossmole, 2005) there is even more options to get relevant data (Cerbo, Dodero & Succi, 2008).There are attempts done to integrate data from various repositories (Conklin, 2007) and various forges are compared for appropriateness (Conklin, 2007; Howison, Wiggins & Crowston, 2008). Influenced by the success of forges in hosting large software projects, there was a proposal of establish Robust Open Source Exchange (ROSE) where developers can prove their identity but remain anonymous for developing enterprise level open source. Since almost everything about FOSS projects are publicly available, there are calls for sharing FOSS research data also (Conklin, 2006).

There are many methods followed in FOSS research including

1. Ethnography (Ducheneaut, Adviser-Sack, Adviser-Lyman, 2003)
2. Case studies (Jensen, Scacchi, 2007)
3. Traditional statistics (Mockus, Fielding, Herbsleb, 2000)
4. Social Network Analysis (Martinez-Romo, Robles, Gonzalez-Barahona, Ortun~o-Perez, 2008)
5. Demographic (Hannemann, Klamma, 2013).

The body of research regarding developmental methodologies in FOSS have traditionally confined to two areas. Firstly, to investigate why talented programmers contribute FOSS and secondly to build models which can explain the devel- opment process in FOSS. Recent research has said that Free and Open software development does not adhere to the traditional engineering rationality found in the legacy of software engineering life-cycle models or prescriptive standards (Madey, G. (n.d.)). Others have demonstrated that FOSS development models offers three interrelated advantages when compared to conventional models: a credible commitment to prevent underinvestment in complementary assets within the value chain, priming the positive-returns network effects cycle, and various efficiency and scale economies(Wikimedia Foundation, Inc., 2017, March 11).

The factors motivating the atop-notch programmers to contribute to FOSS is subjected to intense research. Everyone from Economists to Sociologists is interested in understanding this strange phenomenon. The undeniable economic success of free software has prompted some leading-edge economists to try to understand why many thousands of loosely networked free software developers can compete with Microsoft at its own game and produce a massive operating system GNU Linux (Benkler, 2006). It has been argued that collaborative ideals and principles applied in FOSS projects could be applied to any collaboration built around intellectual property (not just software) and could potentially increase the speed at which innovations and new discoveries are made (Schweik, 2007). Some studies have stated that the motives stem from a mosaic of economic, social and political realms(The R Foundation. (n.d.)). The ideological tilt of the developers towards FOSS and the urge to satisfy their creative instincts are also recognized as prime motivators (Abdullah, 2004; Steven W. (n.d)). Few studies have indicated that altruism is also an important factor that motivates the developers to participate in FOSS projects (Hars, Ou, 2001). For many developers, project code is intellectually stimulating to write. For them, their participation in the FOSS project was their most creative experience or was equally as creative as theirmost creative experience (Lakhani, Wolf, 2005). Some indicate that leaders' transformational leadership is positively related to developers' intrinsic motivation and leaders' active management by exception, a form of transactional leadership, is positivelyrelated to developers' extrinsic motivation (Li, Tan C-Hoo, Hock-Hai, Talib Mattar, 2006).

The first theory regarding development of FOSS was proposed by Eric S Raymond (Raymond, 1999). In his now famous 'Cathedral and the Bazaar' metaphor, he provided the simplistic theory explaining the working of FOSS projects. There have been few attempts to develop new models based on this metaphor (Senyard, Michlmayr, 2004). Lessig Lawrence observed that open code projects, whether free software or opensource software projects share the feature that the knowledge necessary to replicate the project is intended always to be available to others. There is no effort, through law or technology, for the developer of an open code project to make that development exclusive. And, more importantly, the capacity to replicate and redirect the evolution of a project provided in its most efficient form is also always preserved (Lessig, 2006). The model of a sustainable community called 'OnionModel' is also proposed (Aberdour, 2007). Models, which resemble the classic waterfall approach, have also been developed (Yamauchi et al., 2000). The current research in FOSS developmental models hasbeen limited to studying specific FOSS products. Most of these studies have been limited to successful FOSS projects such as Apache, Perl, Sendmail, Mozilla (Lerner & Tirole, 2005; Mockus, Fielding & Herbsleb, 2002).

Not many recognize that the basic principles adopted by the FOSS community were initially proposed by Gerald M. Weinberg (Weinberg, 1998). In his theory of Egoless programming, a technical peer group uses frequent and often peer reviews to find defects in software under development. The objective is for everyone to find defects, including the author, not to prove the work product has no defects. People exchange work products to review, with the expectation that as authors, they will produce errors, and as reviewers, they will find errors. This principle has been put to telling effect by FOSS developers.

There are various studies done on the use of FOSS in critical scientific and business applications. It is said that FOSS is not for hobbyists any more. Instead, it is a business strategy with broad applicability (Krishnamurthy S, (n.d)). In the domain of launch range operations for space vehicle launch, Open-source software offered exciting possibilities for radically shorter development times at substantially lower cost when compared to traditional methods of custom system development (Georgas, Gorlick & Taylor, 2005). The domain of ERP Systems, which maintain the data for a company's main business process have been greatly changed after the introduction of FOSS, based development techniques (Serrano & Sarriegi, 2006).

Academics have been showing keen interest in using FOSS in teaching various Computer Science related courses (Raj & Kazemian, 2006; Toth, 2006; Buchta, Petrenko, Poshyvanyk & Rajlich, 2006). There has even been an attempt to teach FOSS as a part of graduate course (German, 2005). Few colleges have reported how they have used FOSS in developing software to meet their academic requirements (Grob, Bensberg, & Dewanto, 2004; Pastore, 2006).

Several studies have been undertaken to understand the extent of usage and impact of FOSS in several countries or continents. In the study, which spanned entire Europe, it was found that Europe is the leading region in terms of globally collaborating FOSS developers, and leads in terms of global project leaders(Ghosh, 2006). The interest in the FOSS activities in Southeast Finland is also quantified (Nikula & Jantunen, 2005). In an interesting study done on the nature of Open Source adoption in ASEAN member countries (Mindel, Mui & Verma, 2007), it was found that Indonesia has highest rate of FOSS adoption, though the Government there is neutral about this issue. This contrasts the case of Vietnam where FOSS adoption is still low despite the Government there making the use of FOSS mandatory. In September 2003, the Asian trio of China, Japan, and South Korea announced an initiative to promote open source software and platforms that favor non-Microsoft products such as GNU Linux (Chae & McHaney, 2006).

Similar to the research regarding the factors motivating the individuals to con-tribute to FOSS, there has been research into the factors motivating the forms to contribute to FOSS. The companies that join Open Source collaborations are seeking to use the software in a non-differentiating, cost-centerrole (Perens (n.d)). It is found that firms emphasize economic and technological reasons for entering and contributing to Open Source and do not subscribe to many socially-based motivations that are, by contrast, typical of individual programmers. Some companies get into FOSS activities because the user community, which comprises of a very large group of beta testers, allows them to perform a bug fixing better (Nowell & Kleinberg, 2003). Some factors like organizational size, top management support, and availability of resources like limited financial resources, or a pool of FOSS literate IT personnel also enhances the chances of an organization to get into FOSS (Glynn, Fitzgerald & Exton, 2005). A large-scale survey on 146 Italian Open Source firms concluded that intrinsic community based motivations couple with extrinsic, profit-based incentives (Rossi C, Bonaccorsi A, 2005). Some organizations have tried to use FOSS as basic building blocks forcreating mature technologies like operating systems, middleware, databases, protocol stacks and development environments (Ruffin & Ebert, 2004). Some companies have tried to test, certify and integrate FOSS components so that they work together (Goth, 2005). Few have tried to combine FOSS components in their own offerings (Madanmohan & De, 2004). It is argued that large system integrators, or solution providers, stand to gain the most from open source software because they increase profits through direct cost savings and the ability to reach more customers through improved pricing flexibility (Riehle, 2007). Several industry leaders are active in FOSS ecology. IBM and Novell have announced or strengthened their open source offerings from the data server to the desktop, sometimes offering and supporting certified versions of open source applications, sometimes using open source code in new server-based configurations that let customers choose specific functionalities per user (Goth, 2005). IBM, Sun and Apple have experimented with hybrid strategies, which attempted to combine the advantages of open source software while retaining control and differentiation (West, 2003).

There is also some criticism on the commercialization of FOSS projects. There is an argument that this process of commercialization will present some genuine risks to the movement itself. Critics question how these projects which rely onaltruism, ego and pride as the central rewarding mechanisms can continue when these noble efforts are turned into cold, hard cash by enterprising entrepreneur (Neill, 2007).

FOSS RESEARCH TAXONOMY

There have been many attempts to build the taxonomy of FOSS research by Feller and Fitzgerald (Feller & Fitzgerald, 2000), Lerner and Tirole (Lerner & Tirole, 2001), Rossi (Rossi, 2004), Von Krogh and von Hippel (Krogh & Hippel, 2006), Nelson et al. (Nelson, Sen, & Subramaniam, 2006), Niederman et.al (Niederman, Davis, Greiner, Wynn & York, 2006), Scacchi (Scacchi, 2007), Jin et al. (Jin, Robey & Boudreau, 2007) and Aksulu (Aksulu & Wade, 2010). In another study, the major research categories identified are - FOSS communities, FOSS development and maintenance, Diffusion and adoption of FOSS and Characteristics of FOSS. This work also presents a set of 'Guidelines for Reporting Empirical Research in FOSS', which has since been followed in all studies (Stol & Babar, 2009). Another detailed survey of research in FOSS identifies the major research areas as Inputs (Member characteristics, Project characteristics and Technology use), Processes (Software development practices, Social processes and Firm involvement practices), Emergent States (Social states, Task related states) and Outputs (Software implementation, Team performance and Evolution) (Crowston, Wei, Howison & Wiggins, 2012).

Research in FOSS has a relatively short history with the dedicated conference, the International Conference on Open Source Systems having started only in 2005. On the occasion of completion of ten years of the conference, we have studiedthe contributions done by the conference in fostering FOSS research during the past decade. By using the taxonomy originally developed by K. Crowston et al, we have mapped all the papers published in OSS proceedings from 2005 – 2014. A total of 347 papers were classified under the following categories following the original taxonomy. The revised taxonomy can be found in Figure 1. The new categories identified by us are marked as bold and underlined.The papers in each category are listed in further reading section for developer motivation studies.

Figure 1. The revised taxonomy of FOSS research

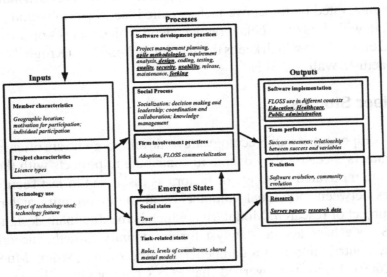

Why should talented software developers work as volunteers in the FOSS development was the first major research question in this domain (Lerner & Tirole, 2002). Surprisingly Weinberg's foretold the answer for this question in his seminal work 'The Psychology of Computer Programming' (Weinberg, 1971). While describing the term "ego-less programming" he said when developers are not territorial about their code, but instead encourage others to improve the systems, improvement is much more likely, widespread and faster. Through the usage of software tools for production and collaboration, laws to distribute and retain the freeness of software, the concept of egoless programming has found its firm place in FOSS development. The six logics of justification suggested by Boltanski and Thevnot, namely - inspirational, domestic, popular, civic, market and industrial logics are used in the context of FOSS (Bergquist, Ljungberg & Rolandsson, 2011).

In a detailed survey of this issue, von Krogh et al, identified three main categories of individual developer motivations in FOSS namely:

1. **Intrinsic Factors:** Ideology, Altruism, Kinship, Fun
2. **Internalised Extrinsic Factors:** Reputation, Reciprocity, Learning, Own use

3.   **Extrinsic Factors:** Career, Pay. They also proposed that even if individuals are motivated by the above factors called 'self determination view' to begin with, it is the 'social practice view' which focuses on social good and unity of life which keeps them going in longterm (Krogh, Haefliger, Spaeth & Wallin, 2012)

Volunteer Studies

The key component of FOSS ecology are its developers who are often labelled as 'volunteers' because they decide to contribute to projects with their free will having motivated by range of factors as discussed in last section. The dynamics between individual volunteers and the community at large has been a subject of research. Modularity, which is the dominant design theme of FOSS code base acts as catalyst for community growth, incentive for voluntary contribution and a dampener for free riding (Milev, Muegge & Weiss, 2009). It has been warned that FOSS community, which although often perceived as a single group, is actually many small groups, each bound by a common interest in a particular piece of software (Schofield & Cooper, 2006). The more successful a project is, the higher is the degree of its complexity in terms of project structure and community size (Hannemann, Liiva & Klamma, 2014). A strong developer base, which sustains for long is important for success of FOSS (Midha, Palvia, 2012; Hannemann & Klamma, 2013). FOSS communities have often been considered to occupy a space between the organized supply of products and services offered by firms and the wider, emergent, market dynamics of software production, supply and demand (Berdou, 2006).

It is important to evaluate the community in order to make sure that project is healthy (Nowell & Kleinberg, 2003). Therefore, there has been a keen interest in studying volunteer contributions in successful projects. Though FOSS promises open participation, most of the projects are maintained by a small set of developers. The performance of the system depends critically on just a small core group of contributors. Increasing that group leads to performance improvement but in a decreasing manner (Levine & Prietula, 2010). Some researchers have argued that Brooks' Law holds true among the core developers of any large FOSS project (Capiluppi & Adams, 2009). It has been found that FreeBSD uses a smaller set of core developers and a larger set of top developers to implement 80 percent of the system (Dinh-Trong & Bieman, 2005). But not all developers stay productive for long. In a study of three major FOSS Bioinformatics projects it was found that only few newbies survive two years after getting initiated into projects. They further note that volunteers who survive longer than three years will survive longer (Hannemann & Klamma, 2013). The support from communities is important not only for development but also for integrating FOSS in organisations (Martinez et al., 2013).

Though FOSS promises open door to everyone it has been found that big, invisible barriers exists here (Steinmacher, Silva & Gerosa, 2014). It is reported that though there are women specific groups like LinuxChix, KDEWomen, UbuntuWomen and DebianWomen (Qiu, Stewart & Bartol, 2010), very few females join and continue in FOSS (Kuechler, Gilbertson & Jensen, 2012). It is also noted that non-technical stakeholders like translators, manual writes and HCI experts are excluded from decision making (Rantalainen, Hedberg & Iivari, 2011). But this claim is refuted by number of further studies where it is reported that communication channels between developers and other experts does exist. And there are good relations between users and developers (Noll, 2007; Iivari, 2010; Bach & Carroll, 2009; Hedberg & Iivari, 2009; Noll, 2008; Kamei et al., 2008).

It is usual to study the distribution licenses in FOSS. But there are another type of license agreement critical to understanding collaboration in FOSS projects: individual contributor license agreements (CLAs) and organizational contributor license agreements (OCLAs), for contributors from organized entities. It is these licenses that serve as contracts for collaboration (Jensen & Scacchi, 2011). When there are differences among developer teams and there is a need for more community driven development, FOSS projects are forked (Robles & Jesus, 2012). Forking does not always impact the project in a wrong way. Fork serves as the invisible hand of sustainability that ensures that code remains open and that the code that best serves the community lives on (Nyman, Mikkonen, Lindman & Foug, 2012).

Though it has been claimed that altruist volunteers primarily drive FOSS there is increasing evidence that many developers are actually paid for their work (Berdou, 2006). Commercial firms are involving in FOSS projects in three ways (models) viz. coding, management and support (Capra, Francalanci, Merlo & Lamastra, 2009). Other researchers have identified three classes of FOSS projects as of date - traditional, industry-involved and industry led (Capiluppi, Stol & Boldyreff, 2012). In a study spanning multiple projects over long period of time it was reported that about 50% of all contributions to projects was paid work (Riehle, Riemer, Kolassa & Schmidt, 2014). Around 6-7% of Debian code is contributed by companies (Robles, Duenas & Gonzalez-

Barahona, 2007). Not surprisingly an author declared commercially viable form of FOSS, namely, OSS2.0 has emerged (Fitzgerald, 2006).

While studying the complex relationship between volunteer driven FOSS projects and commercial organisations it was found that corporate involvement does not necessarily impact the project in a negative way (Jesus, Izquierdo-Cortazar, Maffulli & Robles, 2013; Capiluppi, Baravalle & Heap, 2010). It is suggested, "a major success factor for OSS is the involvement of a commercial company, or more radically, when project management is in hands of a commercial entity" (Capiluppi, Stol & Boldyreff, 2012). The collaboration between the company and the community can, if properly handled, drive a more efficient development (Martinez-Romo, Robles, Gonzalez-Barahona & Ortun~o-Perez, 2008). But it is also noted that outside organizations contribute a majority of code but rarely participate in bug triaging. Their code does not necessarily address the needs of others and may distort governance and direction (Forrest, Jensen, Mohan & Davidson, 2012). Others have found that there is no difference between the paid and volunteer works (Nguyen, Cruzes, Ayala & Conradi, 2011). Integrating new members into the development team is not easy. So it is suggested that companies should handhold the volunteers using existing developers as mentors in the beginning for sustaining them for a longer time (Fagerholm et al., 2014).

Community Studies

Research in the area of FOSS communities has been dominated discussions about governance structure, communication tools used by members and developing 'conceptual integrity' (Brooks, 1975) among the team members. It is often claimed that FOSS developers self-organize into organizational forms (Jensen & Scacchi, 2010). But this is fast changing. As a study reported FOSS development has evoked images of full participation, emancipation and flat organization but recently hierarchical structures have re- emerged in many projects (Seifu & Tsiavos, 2010). A Software Project Governance Framework (SPGF) for FOSS consisting of four elements-contribution, testing, working practices and project leadership has been forwarded (Capra & Wasserman, 2008). In true spirit of openness, emergent leadership is observed in FOSS communities (Crowston, Heckman, Annabi & Masango, 2005).

Extensive survey of communication mechanism between developers and users in FOSS projects are reported (Stol & Babar, 2009). Communication mechanisms used by FOSS developers are also reviewed (Rantalainen, Hedberg & Iivari, 2011)). It is interesting to note that new social media tools like Twitter are also used by FOSS developers (Wang, Kuzmickaja, Stol, Abrahamsson & Fitzgerald, 2013; Lewis, 2013). An important law connecting the communication and architecture styles in an organisation, the Conway's law is studied in FOSS projects (Syeed & Hammouda, 2013).

Though it is known that group learning is necessary for FOSS project to succeed (Annabi & Adviser-Crowston, 2005), it is observed that very few individuals are involved in knowledge sharing processes (Sowe & Stamelos, 2008). An interesting study aimed to use cognitive maps analysis to represent and compare the mental models of the involved members so as to gauge the degree of common knowledge and the development of a collective mind as well as to better understand the reasons that underlie team members actions and the way common mental models, if any, arise (Crowston & Scozzi, 2006).

A major sub-area of research within the community studies is applying Social Network Analysis (SNA) methods to FOSS developers and projects. After the initial attempt in 2002 by Greg Madey (Madey, Freeh & Tynan, 2002), there has been many subsequent attempts in the same direction (Wagstrom, Herbsleb & Carley, 2005; Hahn, Moon & Zhang, 2006; Robertsa, Hann & Slaughter, 2006; Howison, Inoue & Crowston, 2006; Gao & Madey, 2007). While many works focus on the macro level network structures, the social network generated by developers who collaborate on same project, namely, meso level structures are also studied (Conaldi & Rullani, 2010; Jensen & Scacchi, 2010). It is through these studies we learn that FOSS ecology is not a fully connected network. In addition to studying developer collaboration using SNA approaches, it is suggested that code-commit, bug-fixing, mailinglist and code-review data should also bemodelled as social networks for effective analysis (Bosu & Carver, 2014). Further it is noted that the different networks should not be studied in isolation but combined together to make full sense of political nature of FOSS (Ducheneaut, 2005).

SNA methods have resulted in some interesting observations regarding FOSS such as the confirmation of 'rich gets richer' phenomena (Syeed & Hammouda, 2014). Visualising the network data is a challenge due to its huge volume. Hence there is a rich body of work in this area (Balieiro, Junior & Cleidson, 2008; Antwerp & Madey, 2010; Jermakovics, Sillitti & Succi, 2013; Hannemann, Liiva & Klamma, 2014; Azarbakht & Jensen, 2014).

Software Development Studies

The most important differentiator regarding FOSS phenomenon is the development model it practices. It is known to be different from traditional software production in many fundamental aspects (Robles, Duenas & Gonzalez-Barahona, 2007). But aspects like requirement engineering (Scacchi, Jensen, Noll & Elliott, 2005) architectural design (Bass, Kazman & Ozkaya, 2011; Stol, Babar & Avgeriou, 2011), modular design (Narduzzo & Rossi, 2005) and reusability (Capiluppi, Boldyreff & Stol, 2011; Ayala, Søensen, Conradi, Franch & Li, 2007) are found to exist even in FOSS projects but in a different way. Community-orientation, web-based collaborations, peer reviews, short cycle iterations and quick releases are touted as unique practices of FOSS development (Rossi, Russo & Succi, 2009; Jensen & Scacchi, 2010). It is precisely because of these reasons it is often praised for its suit- ability for evolution and adaptation to fast moving demands on software products (Gencer & Øzel, 2012).

Eric Raymond captured the first and well-known characterisation of FOSS development practices in 'Cathedral and Bazaar' metaphor. Though the term has come to mean many things today, what Raymond intended to do in this essay was to sketch a software development process that was used by Linus in development of GNU-Linux and which he employed in a project Fetchmail. It is useful to reorganise his guidelines so that we can correctly interpret what he says regarding the 'bazaar' style of software development. The first issue is how to start aproject.

Here the focus is to find problem at an individual level. The assumption that developer starts the project because he is interested to solve one is too simplistic. In his later essays, Raymond does talk about how one can inherit a project, whichhas been abandoned by its original developer. Whatever the case may be, the initiation into bazaar development model begins with an individual deciding to start a new project or renew an inactive one. Later more developers have to be involved into the project but Raymond is silent about how to attract developers into the project. He however recommends involving more people in the project as opposed to conventional wisdom well known as 'Brookslaw.'

Later he provides guidelines regarding the design and coding of software, which have relevance beyond present discussion on bazaar model. They are in the same league as 'Epigrams on Programming' by Alan Perlis and are worth following eventoday.

The landmark contribution of Raymond while describing bazaar model was his formulation of parallel debugging activities. It is this feature, which has made FOSS so resilient to common problems as witnessed in closed development model. What was initially thought as a sure formula for disaster, the open model of development and testing has proved to be most important aspect of bazaar model. As witnessed by other projects like slashdot and wikipedia, this model of public participation seems to work and Raymond to his credit, identified and codified this practice in an attractive way as follows.

Next, Raymond formulates the most well-known principle of bazaar model relating to release of software. Releasing early precedes the suggestion to rapid release. Unlike what is the popular perception, FOSS projects in bazaar style do not start with a blank sheet. The developer who wants to adopt bazaar model should write an initial stable version and share it with public along with source code and some documentation. Many high-profile projects which did not follow this rule while going bazaar way failed as in the case of Mozilla project. Finally, Raymond gives a solution to the question of longitivity of bazaar project. There are issues of developer burnout, disinterest which can stop the project. In such cases, the developer is encouraged to handover the project to competent successor so that the project does not die.

Overall the 'Cathedral and Bazaar' presents a new model for developers and organisations that want to engage public in software development. But as noted by Raymond, there are certain preconditions for the success of this process. One is the working product, which should be presented to public and second is the leadership style of project coordinator. Without a basic working code, which they can work, and test on, developers will not be inclined to join and contribute to a project. Once the project starts receiving much attention, the leadership style of coordinator determines the fate of the project. Raymond rightly notes that the major contribution of Linus is not actually technical (i.e. the GNU-Linux code) but engineering (i.e managing adiverse set a people for a long period of time). As he poignantly notes 'charming people' seem to get the job done in bazaar model of development.

There has been reassessment of this narrative with one study labelling a phase where the number of active developers and the actual work performed on the system is constant, or does not grow: as 'cathedral'. A phase when sudden growing amount of developers correspond to a similar growing output produced is termed as the 'bazaar' (Capiluppi & Michlmayr, 2007). 'Linus Law' as proposed by Eric Raymond too assume dabi-polar world of developers in FOSS with larger user base also working, as amateur testers will give timely feedback to coders thus creating an efficient system. Many others too found that there are few members in a community who do most of the tasks and many others in periphery who occasionally contribute to project (Fagerholm, Guinea, Sanchez, Borenstein & Mnch, 2014; MacLean, Pratt, Knutson & Ringger, 2011; Terceiro, Rios & Chavez, 2010). But later it was discovered that there are many levels of participation in a FOSS project. This idea was refined and formalised by Kelvin Crowston and colleagues who introduced the next important metaphor regarding FOSS development, namely, 'Onion Model'(Crowston & Howison, 2003).

The onion model is used in many important projects like Linux kernel in a customised manner (Antikainen, Aaltonen & Vaisanen, 2007). Many researchers have attempted refinement of the onion model. The onion model assumes very little interaction between the two groups of volunteers in FOSS community. But it has been shown that the core and the peripheral groups in a project are not isolated but constantly interact with each other and sub groups within (Masmoudi, Besten, Loupy & Dalle, 2009; Scialdone, Li, Heckman & Crowston, 2009). Onion based models are even used measure FOSS communities (Kilamo, Aaltonen & Heinimaki, 2010). The traditional onion model for FOSS communities is substituted with two onions, one for the size of the community and another for the amount of activity on the onion layers (Heinimaki & Aaltonen, 2009).

There have been attempts to give a hierarchical classification of the activities according to prestige scale where coding (rank-1) and bug reporting (rank-6). Unlike the onion model, which only identifies core and periphery volunteers, many roles are identified and social prestige is added to each category (Studer, 2007). Even in Bugzilla, the main activities are found not to be based only on the hierarchical distribution of the work between core and periphery participants but on their implication in the interactions (Masmoudi & Boughzala, 2012). The distinction between two categories is not water-tight and there increasing evidence that participants including periphery developers participate in core activities over time (Heckman et al., 2007). Even the core members evolve over time (Robles, Gonzalez-Barahona & Michlmayr, 2005; Robles & Gonzalez-Barahona, 2006). Through the process of preferential attachment communities add new members, link between communities and migrate between communities (Weiss, Moroiu & Zhao, 2006). In a wonderful analysis of python community, the author describes how developers move from periphery to core. He says it is not simply meritocracy but a complicated political process. Indeed, he makes a powerful statement "OSS development is politics by other means" (Ducheneaut, 2005).

Quality Assurance Studies

If only FOSS projects were limited to hobby market as it was in the initial heady days of hackerdom, quality would not be a major concern. But FOSS has become major component of modern IT infrastructure. Therefore, there are real concerns about the quality of FOSS. Given the fact that it is developed by a loosely connected set of volunteers who interact mainly through Internet and do not follow regimented project management structures, proving the trust-worthiness of FOSS becomes very essential. A quality study is a very active research are within FOSS domain and there are enough evidences to prove that quality assurance practices in FOSS have the potential to deliver reliable software (Michlmayr, Hunt & Probert, 2005; Barham, 2013).

Quality is a very subjective manner. How quality is defined, measured and evaluated is different in traditional and FOSS development. Therefore, it is difficult to apply the same metrics in both cases. As one author notes "Because FOSS projects are evolving, their quality is too, and it must be measured using metrics that take into account its community's commitment to quality rather than just its software structure" (Ruiz & Robinson, 2011). This is the reason while some have found that FOSS applications are slower in responding to quality concerns (Capra, Francalanci & Merlo, 2010; Paulson, Succi & Eberlein, 2004) many others have found they are equal or better than their commercial counterparts (Rigby & Storey, 2011; Michlmayr, Hunt & Probert, 2005; Barham, 2013; Lin & Li, 2014; Ruiz & Robinson, 2011). There are two detailed survey papers in this area (Ruiz & Robinson, 2011; Ahmed, Ghorashi & Jensen, 2014). As FOSS relies mostly on volunteer contribution, this aspect is subjected to much enquiry. It is reported that projects with more core developers don't necessarily have better code quality (Ahmed et al., 2014), it is also noted that more experience does not imply that less buggy code is included in the project (Izquierdo-Corta´zar, Robles & Gonza´lez-Barahona, 2012). The influence of other aspects like product licence (Santos, Kuk, Kon & Pearson, 2013), governance structures (Capra, Francalanci & Merlo, 2008), debugging (Lin & Li, 2014), patches (Sethanandha, Massey & Jones, 2010) and peer review (Rigby & Storey, 2011) on the quality of FOSS are also studied. The popular C&K metrics is also discussed in the context of FOSS (Gyimothy, Ferenc & Siket, 2005; Shatnawi, 2010).

Assessing FOSS by using an established framework and constructing a new framework to evaluate the fitness of FOSS is another fertile area of research. A survey paper in 2010 found twenty FOSS evaluation methods, frameworks and approaches (Stol & Babar, 2010). The popular Capability Maturity Model (CMM) from SEI was initially used to evaluate FOSS (Bleek, Finck & Pape, 2005). Another precursor to maturity models suggested a framework to select the appropriate FOSS project (Ardagna, Damiani, Frati & Reale, 2006). There were also calls to setup a FOSS Quality Observatory (Groot, Kugler, Adams & Gousios, 2006). Portfolio planning method of Boston Consulting Group was adopted to evaluate FOSS projects (Koch & Stix, 2008).

There are many quality models, which primarily emerged from the industry to have a method to evaluate and integrate FOSS products into their offerings. Others have been the result of academic studies. The partial list of quality assessment models in FOSS is given below

1. Open Source Maturity Model (OSMM) from CapGemini
2. Open Source Maturity Model (OSMM) from Navica
3. Business Readiness Rating Project (BRR) (Wasserman, Pal & Chan, 2006)
4. Method for Qualification and Selection of Open Source Software (QSOS) (Semeteys, 2008)
5. Open Business Quality Rating (OpenBQR) (Taibi, Lavazza & Morasca, 2007)
6. SQO-OSS Quality Model (Samoladas, Gousios, Spinellis & Stamelos, 2008)
7. Framework for OS Critical Systems Evaluation (FOCSE) (Ardagna, Damiani & Frati, 2007)
8. Quality Platform for Open Source Software (QualiPSo) (Taibi, Bianco, Carbonare, Lavazza & Morasca, 2008; Bianco, Lavazza, Morasca & Taibi, 2009).

DISCUSSION

The study of a decade of OSS proceedings throws some interesting observations. The locations of the conferences are given in Table 1. It shows that the conference was primarily hosted in Europe with Italy being the favourite choice. Though the conference was held in other continents, it is clear that Europe is turning to be the nerve centre of FOSS research. We understand that choice of location is based on concerns, which are beyond technical. But still it can be inferred that since there is an increased interest and support in Europe

Table 1. Locations and themes of OSS conferences

Year	Location	Theme
2005	Italy	Open Source Systems
2006	Italy	Open Source Systems
2007	Ireland	Open Source Development, Adoption and Innovation
2008	Italy	Open Source Development, Communities and Quality
2009	Sweden	Open Source Ecosystems: Diverse Communities Interacting
2010	USA	Open Source Software: New Horizons
2011	Brazil	Open Source Systems: Grounding Research
2012	Tunisia	Open Source Systems: Long-Term Sustainability
2013	Slovenia	Open Source Software: Quality Verification
2014	Costa Rica	Open Source Software: Mobile Open Source Technologies

for FOSS research and usage, OSS conferences usually locates itself in that continent.

The gradual growth of FOSS research can be understood bystudying thethemes of OSS conferences. Themes serve as aspirational slogans andalso provide research direction. As seen in Table 1, the successiveconferences havefocussed both on introspection and outreach. In the initial years the focus wasnaturally on the consolidation of research area and therefore the themes centredon development, community and quality issues. Later exploring new appli-cation areas ranging from mobile to services of FOSS became the focus. Fromthe beginning relating the research to industry practice has been the hallmark characteristic of the conferences. Exploring the adoption of FOSS in public ad- ministration, health care and education has been another recurring theme in these conferences. Except in 2005 when there was a separate Italian language section, the proceedings of all other years are only in English. Given the huge participa-tion of researchers from non-English speaking world, it is a good point to thinkwhether there is a need to revise the practice of giving space for otherlanguages.

But the significance of a conference is beyond publishing papers. It serves as an opportunity for people with similar thoughts to interact and exchange ideas. The workshops, tutorials, debates, demonstrations, doctoral consortiums, posters and key notes all are equal, if not more, important part of a conference. In this regard, OSS conferences are hugely successful as it had the right mix of all these components. People participating in any of the above-mentioned activities are labelled for the present purpose as

Table 2. Countries of participants

Country	No of Authors	Country	No of Authors
Italy	239	Turkey	11
USA	182	Australia	10
Finland	101	Portugal	10
UK	88	Panama	10
France	79	Austria	8
Spain	75	Denmark	7
Sweden	64	India	5
Japan	44	Israel	5
Brazil	36	Poland	5
Norway	34	Hungary	4
Germany	27	Korea	3
Ireland	26	China	2
Belgium	24	Costa Rica	2
Cuba	24	Iran	2
Greece	24	West Indies	2
Canada	22	Ecuador	1
Netherlands	17	Hong Kong	1
Switzerland	16	Mexico	1
South Africa	12	Singapore	1

participants. The country information of participants is given in Table 2. As in the previous discussion, Italy bags the honour of maximumparticipants with European participants overshadowing all others. USA proves to have strong FOSS research culture and the South American participation is high mainly when the conference moves to that continent. Africa is represented very sparsely and the Asian giants like China and India are under represented. Why is there such a skewed distribution of participation? Is a good research question? Also, this data may provide a basis for organisers to decide the future host of OSS conferences because location seems to have a positive influence on number of contributions from that region.

Table 3 summarises the citation details of papers presented in OSS conferences. It shows that there is a healthy demand for the papers presented here proving that the conference is becoming an important place for reporting

Table 3. Summary of citations

Year	Total Papers	No of Papers Cited	Average Citation	Min Citation	Max Citation
2005	47	45	20.7	1	160
2006	32	29	15.8	2	71
2007	39	37	12.2	1	45
2008	39	36	16.2	1	117
2009	28	28	8.8	1	18
2010	40	30	3.8	1	20
2011	31	22	3.8	1	11
2012	39	22	3.1	1	14
2013	20	12	2.7	1	16
2014	32	7	1.3	1	2

FOSS research. 'OSSmole: A collaborative repository for FLOSS research data and analyses' (Cerbo, Dodero & Succi, 2008) and The Total Growth of Open Source' (Deshpande & Riehle, 2008) are cited more than 100 times. 'Social dynamics of free and open source teamcommunications (Howison, Inoue & Crowston, 2006) is another paper which is hugely cited. More than 90% of papers are cited at least once after five years of publication and this trend increases over time. There is enough scope for future research in this domain. An earlier report (Mulazzani, Rossi, Russo & Steff, 2011) provides an excellent example on how this thread of research can be continued further.

In the course of studying the proceedings of OSS conferences we have observed many interesting anecdotes. The choice of term to refer to the domain seems to strongly favourtowards Open Source today. But in the initial years, researchers alternatively used the terms FOSS, FLOSS and OSS to refer this domain with many authors mentioning the rationale for their choice. We have been able to identify the core team of FOSS researchers reflected by their participation in conference every year. We were able to note the emergence of new research centres in universities focussing on FOSS. Interestingly we were able to track the progress of few researchers from doctoral students to acquiring faculty positions and also notice the change in universities of few researchers. These detailshelped us connect to FOSS research at a more personal level.

CONCLUSION

The present chapter traced the emergence and growth of the FOSS and the related research. The analysis of the papers intended to understand the impact of OSS conferences on FOSS research. Developing a comprehensive taxonomy forFOSS research is an important step as it signals the maturity of the domain. After evaluating existing taxonomies, it was decided to extend an existing one by adding more categories. This revised taxonomy was used to classify the 347 full and short papers presented in the conferences. The classification demonstrates the areas, which attract more attention from researchers. The chronological ordering of papers is helpful to trace the evolution of research themes over time. The analysis of location and themes of conferences provide new insights. Study of participants suggests that the phenomenon is limited to few places. Citation analysis demonstrates the healthy trend of FOSS research. Overall, this work documents the current state of FOSS research.

REFERENCES

Hess, C., & Ostrom, E. (2005). A Framework for Analyzing the Knowledge Commons. In *Understanding Knowledge as a Commons Theory into Practice*. Academic Press.

Schweik, C. M. (2007). Free/open-source software as a framework for establishing commons in science. *Understanding Knowledge as a Commons, 277.*

Berdou, E., & Dini, P. (2005). *Report on the socio-economics of Free/Open Source*. DBE.

Aberdour, M. (2007). Achieving quality in open-source software. *IEEE Software, 24*(1), 58–64. doi:10.1109/MS.2007.2

Ahmed, I., Ghorashi, S., & Jensen, C. (2014, May). *An Exploration of Code Quality in FOSS Projects*. OSS. doi:10.1007/978-3-642-55128-4_26

Aksulu, A., & Wade, M. (2010). A comprehensive review and synthesis of open source research. *Journal of the Association for Information Systems, 11*(11), 576.

Anthony, D., Smith, S. W., & Williamson, T. (2005). *Explaining quality in internet collective goods: Zealots and good samaritans in the case of wikipedia*. Dartmouth College.

Antikainen, M., Aaltonen, T., & Väisänen, J. (2007). The role of trust in OSS communities—case Linux Kernel community. *Open Source Development, Adoption and Innovation, 223-228.*

Ardagna, C., Damiani, E., Frati, F., & Reale, S. (2006). Adopting open source for mission-critical applications: A case study on single sign-on.*Open Source Systems*, 209-220.

Ardagna, C. A., Damiani, E., & Frati, F. (2007, June). FOCSE: An OWA-based Evaluation Framework for OS Adoption in Critical Environments. In *IFIP International Conference on Open Source Systems* (pp. 3-16). Springer. doi:10.1007/978-0-387-72486-7_1

Ayala, C., Cruzes, D., Nguyen, A., Conradi, R., Franch, X., Höst, M., & Babar, M. (2012). OSS integration issues and community support: An integrator perspective. *Open Source Systems: Long-Term Sustainability*, 129-143.

Ayala, C., Søensen, C. F., Conradi, R., Franch, X., & Li, J. (2007). Open source collaboration for fostering off-the-shelf components selection. *Open Source Development, Adoption and Innovation*, 17-30.

Azarbakht, A., & Jensen, C. (2014, May). Drawing the Big Picture: Temporal Visualization of Dynamic Collaboration Graphs of OSS Software Forks. In OSS (pp. 41-50). Academic Press.

Bach, P. M., & Carroll, J. M. (2009, June). FLOSS UX design: An analysis of user experience design in Firefox and OpenOffice. org. In *IFIP International Conference on Open Source Systems* (pp. 237-250). Springer. doi:10.1007/978-3-642-02032-2_21

Balieiro, M. A., de Júnior, S. F. S., & De Souza, C. R. (2008, September). Facilitating social network studies of FLOSS using the OSSNetwork environment. In *IFIP International Conference on Open Source Systems* (pp. 343-350). Springer US. doi:10.1007/978-0-387-09684-1_31

Banzi, M., Bruno, G., & Caire, G. (2008, September). To what extent does it pay to approach open source software for a big telco player? In *IFIP International Conference on Open Source Systems* (pp. 307-315). Springer. doi:10.1007/978-0-387-09684-1_27

Barham, A. (2013, June). The Emergence of Quality Assurance Practices in Free/Libre Open Source Software: A Case Study. In *IFIP International Conference on Open Source Systems* (pp. 271-276). Springer. doi:10.1007/978-3-642-38928-3_21

Bass, L., Kazman, R., & Ozkaya, I. (2011, October). Developing architectural documentation for the hadoop distributed file system. In *IFIP International Conference on Open Source Systems* (pp. 50-61). Springer Berlin Heidelberg. doi:10.1007/978-3-642-24418-6_4

Benkler, Y. (2006). *The wealth of networks: How social production transforms markets and freedom.* Yale University Press.

Benkler, Y., & Nissenbaum, H. (2006). Commons-based peer production and virtue. *Journal of Political Philosophy*, *14*(4), 394–419. doi:10.1111/j.1467-9760.2006.00235.x

Berdou, E. (2006, June). Insiders and outsiders: paid contributors and the dynamics of cooperation in community led F/OS projects. In *IFIP International Conference on Open Source Systems* (pp. 201-208). Springer. doi:10.1007/0-387-34226-5_20

Bergquist, M., Ljungberg, J., & Rolandsson, B. (2011). A historical account of the value of free and open source software: From software commune to commercial commons. *Open Source Systems: Grounding Research*, 196-207.

Bleek, W. G., Finck, M., & Pape, B. (2005, July). Towards an open source development process? Evaluating the migration to an open source project by means of the capability maturity model. In *Proceedings of the First International Conference on Open Source Systems* (pp. 37-43). Academic Press.

Boccacci, P., Carrega, V., & Dodero, G. (2007, June). Open source technologies for visually impaired people. In *IFIP International Conference on Open Source Systems* (pp. 241-246). Springer US. doi:10.1007/978-0-387-72486-7_22

Bodie, M. (2007). The future of the casebook: An argument for an open-source approach. *Journal of Legal Education*, *57*(1), 10–35.

Brink, D., Roos, L., Weller, J., & Van Belle, J. P. (2006). Critical success factors for migrating to OSS-on-the-desktop: common themes across three South African case studies. *Open Source Systems*, 287-293.

Buchta, J., Petrenko, M., Poshyvanyk, D., & Rajlich, V. (2006, September). Teaching evolution of open-source projects in software engineering courses. In *Software Maintenance, 2006. ICSM '06. 22nd IEEE International Conference on* (pp. 136-144). IEEE. doi:10.1109/ICSM.2006.66

Capiluppi, A., & Adams, P. (2009). Reassessing Brooks' law for the free software community. *Open Source Ecosystems: Diverse Communities Interacting*, 274-283.

Capiluppi, A., Boldyreff, C., & Stol, K. J. (2011). Successful reuse of software components: A report from the open source perspective. *Open Source Systems: Grounding Research*, 159-176.

Capiluppi, A., & Michlmayr, M. (2007). From the cathedral to the bazaar: An empirical study of the lifecycle of volunteer community projects. *Open Source Development, Adoption and Innovation*, 31-44.

Capiluppi, A., Stol, K. J., & Boldyreff, C. (2012). *Exploring the role of commercial stakeholders in open source software evolution*. Academic Press.

Capra, E., Francalanci, C., & Merlo, F. (2008). An empirical study on the relationship between software design quality, development effort and governance in open source projects. *IEEE Transactions on Software Engineering*, *34*(6), 765–782. doi:10.1109/TSE.2008.68

Capra, E., Francalanci, C., & Merlo, F. (2010). The economics of community open source software projects: An empirical analysis of maintenance effort. *Advances in Software Engineering*.

Capra, E., Francalanci, C., Merlo, F., & Lamastra, C. R. (2009, June). A survey on firms' participation in open source community projects. In *IFIP International Conference on Open Source Systems* (pp. 225-236). Springer. doi:10.1007/978-3-642-02032-2_20

Chae, B. K., & McHaney, R. (2006). Asian trio's adoption of Linux-based open source development. *Communications of the ACM*, *49*(9), 95–99. doi:10.1145/1151030.1151035

Conklin, M. (2006). Beyond low-hanging fruit: SEEKING the next generation in floss data mining. *Open Source Systems*, 47-56.

Conklin, M. (2007, June). Project entity matching across floss repositories. In *IFIP International Conference on Open Source Systems* (pp. 45-57). Springer.

Crowston, K., & Howison, J. (2003). *The social structure of open source software development teams*. Academic Press.

Davini, E., Faggioni, E., & Tartari, D. (2005, July). Open Source Software in Public Administration. A real example OSS for e-government Observatories. In *First International Conference on Open Source Systems* (pp. 119-124). Academic Press.

Davis, A. R., Niederman, F., Greiner, M. E., Wynn, D., & York, P. T. (2006). A research agenda for studying open source I: A multi-level framework. *Communications of the Association for Information Systems, 18*(7), 129.

Dawid, W. (2005). *Quantitative analysis of open source projects on sourceforge*. Academic Press.

De Groot, A., Kügler, S., Adams, P., & Gousios, G. (2006). Call for quality: Open source software quality observation. *Open Source Systems*, 57-62.

Del Bianco, V., Lavazza, L., Morasca, S., & Taibi, D. (2009). Quality of open source software: the QualiPSo Trustworthiness Model. *Open Source Ecosystems: Diverse Communities Interacting*, 199-212.

Dewanto, B. L., Grob, H. L., & Bensberg, F. (2004). Developing, deploying, using and evaluating an open source learning management system. *CIT. Journal of Computing and Information Technology, 12*(2), 127–134. doi:10.2498/cit.2004.02.08

Dinh-Trong, T. T., & Bieman, J. M. (2005). The FreeBSD project: A replication case study of open source development. *IEEE Transactions on Software Engineering, 31*(6), 481–494. doi:10.1109/TSE.2005.73

Dobusch, L. (2008). Migration discourse structures: Escaping Microsoft's desktop path. *Open Source Development, Communities and Quality*, 223-235.

Ducheneaut, N. (2003). *The reproduction of Open Source software programming communities*. University of California at Berkeley.

Ducheneaut, N. (2005). Socialization in an open source software community: A socio-technical analysis. *Computer Supported Cooperative Work, 14*(4), 323–368. doi:10.1007/s10606-005-9000-1

Fagerholm, F., Guinea, A. S., Borenstein, J., & Münch, J. (2014). Onboarding in open source projects. *IEEE Software, 31*(6), 54–61. doi:10.1109/MS.2014.107

Feller, J., & Fitzgerald, B. (2000, December). A framework analysis of the open source software development paradigm. In *Proceedings of the twenty first international conference on Information systems* (pp. 58-69). Association for Information Systems.

Fitzgerald, B. (2006). The transformation of open source software. *Management Information Systems Quarterly*, 587–598.

Gamalielsson, J., & Lundell, B. (2012). Long-term sustainability of open source software communities beyond a fork: A case study of libreoffice. *Open Source Systems: Long-Term Sustainability*, 29-47.

Garbett, A., Lieser, K., & Boldyreff, C. (2010). Collaborative Development for the XO Laptop: CODEX 2. In *Open Source Software*. New Horizons.

Gençer, M., & Özel, B. (2012). Forking the commons: Developmental tensions and evolutionary patterns in open source software. *Open Source Systems: Long-Term Sustainability*, 310-315.

Georgas, J. C., Gorlick, M. M., & Taylor, R. N. (2005, May). Raging incrementalism: Harnessing change with open-source software. *Software Engineering Notes*, *30*(4), 1–6.

German, M. D. (2005, July). Experiences teaching a graduate course in open source software engineering. In *Proceedings of the first International Conference on Open Source Systems* (pp. 326-328). Academic Press.

Ghosh, R. A. (2006). *Study on the: Economic impact of open source software on innovation and the competitiveness of the Information and Communication Technologies (ICT) sector in the EU*. Bericht für die Europäische Kommission.

Glynn, E., Fitzgerald, B., & Exton, C. (2005, November). Commercial adoption of open source software: an empirical study. In *Empirical Software Engineering, 2005. 2005 International Symposium on*. IEEE. doi:10.1109/ISESE.2005.1541831

Gök, A. (2004). *Open source versus proprietary software: An economic perspective*. Retrieved from open.bilgi.edu. tr/freedays_2004/papers/Abdullah_Gok.pdf

Goñi, A., Boodraj, M., & Cabreja, Y. (2014, January). *A Methodology for Managing FOSS Migration Projects*. OSS.

Goth, G. (2005). Open source business models: Ready for prime time. *IEEE Software*, *22*(6), 98–100. doi:10.1109/MS.2005.157

Goth, G. (2005). Open source meets venture capital. *IEEE Distributed Systems Online*, *6*(6), 2. doi:10.1109/MDSO.2005.33

Gyimothy, T., Ferenc, R., & Siket, I. (2005). Empirical validation of object-oriented metrics on open source software for fault prediction. *IEEE Transactions on Software Engineering*, *31*(10), 897–910. doi:10.1109/ TSE.2005.112

Hannemann, A., & Klamma, R. (2013, June). Community dynamics in open source software projects: Aging and social reshaping. In *IFIP International Conference on Open Source Systems* (pp. 80-96). Springer. doi:10.1007/978-3-642-38928-3_6

Hannemann, A., Liiva, K., & Klamma, R. (2014, May). *Navigation Support in Evolving Open-Source Communities by a Web-Based Dashboard*. OSS. doi:10.1007/978-3-642-55128-4_2

Hardy, J. L., & Bourgois, M. (2006). Exploring the potential of OSS in Air Traffic Management. *Open Source Systems*, 173-179.

Hars, A., & Ou, S. (2001, January). Working for free? Motivations of participating in open source projects. In *System Sciences, 2001. Proceedings of the 34th Annual Hawaii International Conference on* (pp. 9-pp). IEEE. doi:10.1109/HICSS.2001.927045

Hauge, Ø., & Ziemer, S. (2009). Providing Commercial Open Source Software: Lessons Learned. *Open Source Ecosystems: Diverse Communities Interacting*, 70-82.

Heckman, R., Crowston, K., Eseryel, U. Y., Howison, J., Allen, E., & Li, Q. (2007, June). Emergent decision-making practices in free/libre open source software (FLOSS) development teams. In *IFIP International Conference on Open Source Systems* (pp. 71-84). Springer. doi:10.1007/978-0-387-72486-7_6

Hedberg, H., & Iivari, N. (2009). Integrating HCI specialists into open source software development projects. *Open Source Ecosystems: Diverse Communities Interacting*, 251-263.

Heinimäki, T. J., & Aaltonen, T. (2009). An onion is not enough-Living in the multi-onion world. *Proceedings of the Open Source Workshop OSW 2009. Open Source Workshop (OSW 2009)*.

Henttonen, K. (2011). Libre Software as an Innovation Enabler in India Experiences of a Bangalorian Software SME. *Open Source Systems: Grounding Research*, 220-232.

Howison, J., Wiggins, A., & Crowston, K. (2008). eResearch workflows for studying free and open source software development. *Open Source Development, Communities and Quality*, 405-411.

Iivari, N. (2010, May). Usability Innovations in OSS Development–Examining User Innovations in an OSS Usability Discussion Forum. In *IFIP International Conference on Open Source Systems* (pp. 119-129). Springer. doi:10.1007/978-3-642-13244-5_10

Izquierdo-Cortázar, D., Robles, G., & González-Barahona, J. (2012). Do more experienced developers introduce fewer bugs?. *Open Source Systems: Long-Term Sustainability*, 268-273.

Jaaksi, A. (2007). Experiences on product development with open source software. *International Federation for Information Processing*, *234*, 85–96. doi:10.1007/978-0-387-72486-7_7

Jensen, C., & Scacchi, W. (2007, May). Role migration and advancement processes in OSSD projects: A comparative case study. In *Software Engineering, 2007. ICSE 2007. 29th International Conference on* (pp. 364-374). IEEE. doi:10.1109/ICSE.2007.74

Jensen, C., & Scacchi, W. (2010). Governance in open source software development projects: A comparative multi-level analysis. *Open Source Software: New Horizons*, 130-142.

Jermakovics, A., Sillitti, A., & Succi, G. (2013, June). Exploring collaboration networks in open-source projects. In *IFIP International Conference on Open Source Systems* (pp. 97-108). Springer.

Jin, L., Robey, D., & Boudreau, M. C. (2007). Beyond development: A research agenda for investigating open source software user communities. *Information Resources Management Journal*, *20*(1), 68–80. doi:10.4018/irmj.2007010105

Kamei, Y., Matsumoto, S., Maeshima, H., Onishi, Y., Ohira, M., & Matsumoto, K. I. (2008, September). Analysis of coordination between developers and users in the apache community. In *IFIP International Conference on Open Source Systems* (pp. 81-92). Springer. doi:10.1007/978-0-387-09684-1_7

Kilamo, T., Aaltonen, T., & Heinimäki, T. J. (2010, May). BULB: Onion-based measuring of OSS communities. In *IFIP International Conference on Open Source Systems* (pp. 342-347). Springer.

Kilamo, T., Hammouda, I., Kairamo, V., Räsänen, P., & Saarinen, J. P. (2012, September). *Open Source, Open Innovation and Intellectual Property Rights-A Lightning Talk*. OSS. doi:10.1007/978-3-642-33442-9_25

Koch, S. (2005, July). Evolution of open source software systems–a large-scale investigation. *Proceedings of the 1st International Conference on Open Source Systems*.

Koch, S., & Stix, V. (2008). Open source project categorization based on growth rate analysis and portfolio planning methods. *Open Source Development, Communities and Quality*, 375-380.

Koch, S., Strecker, S., & Frank, U. (2006, June). Conceptual modelling as a new entry in the bazaar: The open model approach. In *IFIP International Conference on Open Source Systems* (pp. 9-20). Springer. doi:10.1007/0-387-34226-5_2

Krishnamurthy, S. (2005). *An analysis of open source business models*. Retrieved from http://faculty.washington.edu/sandeep/d/bazaar.pdf

Kuechler, V., Gilbertson, C., & Jensen, C. (2012, September). Gender differences in early free and open source software joining process. In *IFIP International Conference on Open Source Systems* (pp. 78-93). Springer. doi:10.1007/978-3-642-33442-9_6

Lakhani, K. R., & Wolf, R. G. (2005). Why hackers do what they do: Understanding motivation and effort in free/open source software projects. *Perspectives on Free and Open Source Software, 1*, 3-22.

Lakka, S., Stamati, T., & Martakos, D. (2012, September). Does OSS Affect E-Government Growth? An Econometric Analysis on the Impacting Factors. In OSS (pp. 292-297). Academic Press.

Lerner, J., & Tirole, J. (2001). The open source movement: Key research questions. *European Economic Review, 45*(4), 819–826. doi:10.1016/S0014-2921(01)00124-6

Lerner, J., & Tirole, J. (2002). Some simple economics of open source. *The Journal of Industrial Economics, 50*(2), 197–234. doi:10.1111/1467-6451.00174

Lerner, J., & Tirole, J. (2004). Economic perspectives on open source. In *Intellectual Property and Entrepreneurship* (pp. 33–69). Emerald Group Publishing Limited. doi:10.1016/S1048-4736(04)01502-4

Lessig, L. (2009). *Code: And other laws of cyberspace*. ReadHowYouWant. com.

Levine, S. S., & Prietula, M. J. (2010, May). Where and When Can Open Source Thrive? Towards a Theory of Robust Performance. In *IFIP International Conference on Open Source Systems* (pp. 156-176). Springer. doi:10.1007/978-3-642-13244-5_13

Li, Y., Tan, C. H., Teo, H. H., & Mattar, A. T. (2006, April). Motivating open source software developers: influence of transformational and transactional leaderships. In *Proceedings of the 2006 ACM SIGMIS CPR conference on computer personnel research: Forty four years of computer personnel research: achievements, challenges & the future* (pp. 34-43). ACM. doi:10.1145/1125170.1125182

Liben-Nowell, D., & Kleinberg, J. (2007). The link-prediction problem for social networks. *Journal of the Association for Information Science and Technology, 58*(7), 1019-1031.

Lin, C. T., & Li, Y. F. (2014). Rate-based queueing simulation model of open source software debugging activities. *IEEE Transactions on Software Engineering, 40*(11), 1075–1099. doi:10.1109/TSE.2014.2354032

Lindman, J., Rossi, M., & Marttiin, P. (2008, September). Applying open source development practices inside a company. In *IFIP International Conference on Open Source Systems* (pp. 381-387). Springer. doi:10.1007/978-0-387-09684-1_36

Lorenzi, D., & Rossi, C. (2008). Assessing innovation in the software sector: proprietary vs. FOSS production mode. Preliminary evidence from the Italian case. *Open Source Development, Communities and Quality*, 325-331.

Lundell, B., Lings, B., & Lindqvist, E. (2006). Perceptions and uptake of open source in Swedish organisations. *International Federation for Information Processing, 203*, 155–163. doi:10.1007/0-387-34226-5_15

Lundell, B., & Lings, B. (2010). How open are local government documents in Sweden? A case for open standards. *Open Source Software: New Horizons*, 177-187.

MacLean, A. C., Pratt, L. J., Knutson, C. D., & Ringger, E. K. (2011, October). Knowledge homogeneity and specialization in the Apache HTTP Server project. In *IFIP International Conference on Open Source Systems* (pp. 106-122). Springer. doi:10.1007/978-3-642-24418-6_8

Madanmohan, T. R., & Rahul De', . (2004). Notice of violation of IEEE publication principles open source reuse in commercial firms. *IEEE Software*, *21*(6), 62–69. doi:10.1109/MS.2004.45

Madey, G. (2017, March 11). *SourceForge.net Research Data*. Retrieved March 11, 2017, from http://www3.nd.edu/~oss/Data/data.html

Martinez-Romo, J., Robles, G., Gonzalez-Barahona, J. M., & Ortuño-Perez, M. (2008, September). Using social network analysis techniques to study collaboration between a FLOSS community and a company. In *IFIP International Conference on Open Source Systems* (pp. 171-186). Springer. doi:10.1007/978-0-387-09684-1_14

Masmoudi, H., & Boughzala, I. (2012). A Linguistic Analysis on How Contributors Solve Software Problems in a Distributed Context. *Open Source Systems: Long-Term Sustainability*, 322-330.

Masmoudi, H., Den Besten, M., De Loupy, C., & Dalle, J. M. (2009, June). Peeling the onion. In *IFIP International Conference on Open Source Systems* (pp. 284-297). Springer.

Melian, C., & Mähring, M. (2008, September). Lost and gained in translation: Adoption of open source software development at Hewlett-Packard. In *IFIP International Conference on Open Source Systems* (pp. 93-104). Springer US. doi:10.1007/978-0-387-09684-1_8

Michlmayr, M., Hunt, F., & Probert, D. (2005, July). Quality practices and problems in free software projects. In *Proceedings of the First International Conference on Open Source Systems* (pp. 24-28). Academic Press.

Midha, V., & Palvia, P. (2012). Factors affecting the success of Open Source Software. *Journal of Systems and Software*, *85*(4), 895–905. doi:10.1016/j.jss.2011.11.010

Milev, R., Muegge, S., & Weiss, M. (2009). Design evolution of an open source project using an improved modularity metric. *Open Source Ecosystems: Diverse Communities Interacting*, 20-33.

Mindel, J. L., Mui, L., & Verma, S. (2007, January). Open Source Software adoption in ASEAN member countries. In *System Sciences, 2007. HICSS 2007. 40th Annual Hawaii International Conference on* (pp. 226b-226b). IEEE. doi:10.1109/HICSS.2007.412

Mockus, A., Fielding, R. T., & Herbsleb, J. (2000, June). A case study of open source software development: the Apache server. In *Software Engineering, 2000. Proceedings of the 2000 International Conference on* (pp. 263-272). IEEE. doi:10.1145/337180.337209

Mockus, A., Fielding, R. T., & Herbsleb, J. D. (2002). Two case studies of open source software development: Apache and Mozilla. *ACM Transactions on Software Engineering and Methodology*, *11*(3), 309–346. doi:10.1145/567793.567795

Mulazzani, F., Rossi, B., Russo, B., & Steff, M. (2011). Building knowledge in open source software research in six years of conferences. *Open Source Systems: Grounding Research*, 123-141.

Narduzzo, A., & Rossi, A. (2003). Modular design and the development of complex artifacts: Lessons from free/open source software. *Quaderno, DISA, 78*.

Neill, C. J. (2007). Will Commercialization of Open Source Drive the Volunteers Away? *IT Professional Magazine*, *9*(1), 51–53. doi:10.1109/MITP.2007.22

Nelson, M., Sen, R., & Subramaniam, C. (2006). Understanding open source software: A research classification framework. *Communications of the Association for Information Systems*, *17*(1), 12.

Nikula, U., & Jantunen, S. (2005, June). Quantifying the interest in open source system: case south-east Finland. In *Proceedings of the 1st International Conference on Open Source Systems* (pp. 192-95). Academic Press.

Noda, T., & Tansho, T. (2010). Open Source Introducing Policy and Promotion of Regional Industries in Japan. *Open Source Software: New Horizons*, 214-223.

Noda, T., & Tansho, T. (2014, May). *A Study of the Effect on Business Growth by Utilization and Contribution of Open Source Software in Japanese IT Companies*. OSS. doi:10.1007/978-3-642-55128-4_32

Noda, T., Tansho, T., & Coughlan, S. (2013, June). Effect on Business Growth by Utilization and Contribution of Open Source Software in Japanese IT Companies. In *IFIP International Conference on Open Source Systems* (pp. 222-231). Springer. doi:10.1007/978-3-642-38928-3_16

Noll, J. (2007). Innovation in open source software development: A tale of two features. *Open Source Development, Adoption and Innovation*, 109-120.

Noll, J. (2008). Requirements acquisition in open source development: Firefox 2.0. *Open Source Development, Communities and Quality*, 69-79.

Nyman, L., Mikkonen, T., Lindman, J., & Fougère, M. (2012). Perspectives on Code Forking and Sustainability in Open Source Software. *Open Source Systems: Long-Term Sustainability*, 274-279.

Pastore, S. (2006, August). Web Content Management Systems: using Plone open source software to build a website for research institute needs. In *Digital Telecommunications, 2006. ICDT'06. International Conference on* (pp. 24-24). IEEE. doi:10.1109/ICDT.2006.81

Paulson, J. W., Succi, G., & Eberlein, A. (2004). An empirical study of open-source and closed-source software products. *IEEE Transactions on Software Engineering*, *30*(4), 246–256. doi:10.1109/TSE.2004.1274044

Perens, B. (2005). The emerging economic paradigm of open source. *First Monday*. Retrieved from http://www.firstmonday.org/issues/special1010/perens/index.htm

Pfaff, C., & Hasan, H. (2007). Can Knowledge Management be Open Source? *Open Source Development, Adoption and Innovation*, 59-70.

Pinto, G., & Kamei, F. (2014, May). The census of the brazilian open-source community. In *IFIP International Conference on Open Source Systems* (pp. 202-211). Springer. doi:10.1007/978-3-642-55128-4_30

Pratt, L., MacLean, A., Knutson, C., & Ringger, E. (2011). Cliff walls: An analysis of monolithic commits using latent dirichlet allocation. *Open Source Systems: Grounding Research*, 282-298.

Qiu, Y., Stewart, K., & Bartol, K. (2010). Joining and socialization in open source women's groups: an exploratory study of KDE-Women. *Open Source Software: New Horizons*, 239-251.

Quezada, B. J. P., & Fernández, J. (2014, May). Automation of Agricultural Irrigation System with Open Source. In *IFIP International Conference on Open Source Systems* (pp. 232-233). Springer. doi:10.1007/978-3-642-55128-4_36

Rainer, A., & Gale, S. (2005). Evaluating the quality and quantity of data on open source software projects. *Procs 1st Int Conf on Open Source Software.*

Raj, R. K., & Kazemian, F. (2006, October). Using open source software in computer science courses. In *Frontiers in Education Conference, 36th Annual* (pp. 21-26). IEEE. doi:10.1109/FIE.2006.322357

Rantalainen, A., Hedberg, H., & Iivari, N. (2011). A review of tool support for user-related communication in FLOSS development. *Open Source Systems: Grounding Research*, 90-105.

Ravesteyn, P., & Silvius, G. (2008, September). Willingness to cooperate within the open source software domain. In *IFIP International Conference on Open Source Systems* (pp. 367-373). Springer. doi:10.1007/978-0-387-09684-1_34

Raymond, E. (1999). The cathedral and the bazaar. *Philosophy & Technology*, *12*(3), 23.

Riehle, D. (2007). The economic motivation of open source software: Stakeholder perspectives. *Computer*, *40*(4), 25–32. doi:10.1109/MC.2007.147

Riehle, D., Riemer, P., Kolassa, C., & Schmidt, M. (2014, January). Paid vs. volunteer work in open source. In *System Sciences (HICSS), 2014 47th Hawaii International Conference on* (pp. 3286-3295). IEEE. doi:10.1109/HICSS.2014.407

Rigby, P. C., & Storey, M. A. (2011, May). Understanding broadcast based peer review on open source software projects. In *Proceedings of the 33rd International Conference on Software Engineering* (pp. 541-550). ACM. doi:10.1145/1985793.1985867

Ripley, B. D. (2001). The R project in statistical computing. *MSOR Connections. The newsletter of the LTSN Maths. Stats & OR Network*, *1*(1), 23–25.

Robles, G., Duenas, S., & Gonzalez-Barahona, J. M. (2007, June). Corporate involvement of libre software: Study of presence in Debian code over time. In *IFIP International Conference on Open Source Systems* (pp. 121-132). Springer. doi:10.1007/978-0-387-72486-7_10

Robles, G., & González-Barahona, J. (2012). A comprehensive study of software forks: Dates, reasons and outcomes. *Open Source Systems: Long-Term Sustainability*, 1-14.

Robles, G., Gonzalez-Barahona, J. M., & Michlmayr, M. (2005, July). Evolution of volunteer participation in libre software projects: evidence from Debian. In *Proceedings of the 1st international conference on open source systems* (pp. 100-107). Academic Press.

Rossi, C., & Bonaccorsi, A. (2005, May). Why profit-oriented companies enter the OS field?: Intrinsic vs. extrinsic incentives. *Software Engineering Notes*, *30*(4), 1–5. doi:10.1145/1082983.1083269

Rossi, M. A. (2004). *Decoding the "free/open Source (F/OSS) Software Puzzle", a Survey of Theoretical and Empirical Contributions*. Academic Press.

Ruffin, C., & Ebert, C. (2004). Using open source software in product development: A primer. *IEEE Software*, *21*(1), 82–86. doi:10.1109/MS.2004.1259227

Ruiz, C., & Robinson, W. (2011). Towards a Unified Definition of Open Source Quality. *Open Source Systems: Grounding Research*, 17-33.

Samoladas, I., Gousios, G., Spinellis, D., & Stamelos, I. (2008). The SQO-OSS quality model: measurement based open source software evaluation. *Open Source Development, Communities and Quality*, 237-248.

Santos, C., Kuk, G., Kon, F., & Pearson, J. (2013). The attraction of contributors in free and open source software projects. *The Journal of Strategic Information Systems*, *22*(1), 26–45. doi:10.1016/j.jsis.2012.07.004

Scacchi, W. (2005). Socio-technical interaction networks in free/open source software development processes. In Software Process Modeling (pp. 1-27). Springer US.

Scacchi, W. (2007). Free/open source software development: Recent research results and methods. *Advances in Computers*, *69*, 243–295. doi:10.1016/S0065-2458(06)69005-0

Scacchi, W. (2011). Modding as an open source approach to extending computer game systems. *Open Source Systems: Grounding Research*, 62-74.

Scacchi, W., Jensen, C., Noll, J., & Elliott, M. (2005, June). Multi-modal modeling of open source software requirements processes. In *First International Conference on Open Source Systems* (pp. 1-8). Academic Press.

Schofield, A., & Cooper, G. (2006). Participation in Free and Open Source Communities: An Empirical Study of Community Members' Perceptions. *Open Source Systems*, 221-231.

Schweik, C. M. (2007). Free/open-source software as a framework for establishing commons in science. *Understanding Knowledge as a Commons*, 277.

Scialdone, M., Li, N., Heckman, R., & Crowston, K. (2009). Group maintenance behaviors of core and peripherial members of free/libre open source software teams. *Open Source Ecosystems: Diverse Communities Interacting*, 298-309.

Semeteys, R. (2008, May). Method for qualification and selection of open source software. *Open Source Business Resource*.

Senyard, A., & Michlmayr, M. (2004, November). How to have a successful free software project. In *Software Engineering Conference, 2004. 11th Asia-Pacific* (pp. 84-91). IEEE. doi:10.1109/APSEC.2004.58

Serrano, N., & Sarriei, J. M. (2006). Open source software ERPs: A new alternative for an old need. *IEEE Software*, *23*(3), 94–97. doi:10.1109/MS.2006.78

Sethanandha, B. D., Massey, B., & Jones, W. (2010, July). Managing open source contributions for software project sustainability. In *Technology Management for Global Economic Growth (PICMET), 2010 Proceedings of PICMET'10:* (pp. 1-9). IEEE.

Shatnawi, R. (2010). A quantitative investigation of the acceptable risk levels of object-oriented metrics in open-source systems. *IEEE Transactions on Software Engineering*, *36*(2), 216–225. doi:10.1109/TSE.2010.9

Sowe, S., Angelis, L., Stamelos, I., & Manolopoulos, Y. (2007). Using Repository of Repositories (RoRs) to study the growth of F/OSS projects: A meta-analysis research approach. *Open Source Development, Adoption and Innovation*, 147-160.

Sowe, S. K., & McNaughton, M. (2012, September). Using Multiple Case Studies to Analyse Open Source Software Business Sustainability in Sub-Saharan Africa. In *IFIP International Conference on Open Source Systems* (pp. 160-177). Springer. doi:10.1007/978-3-642-33442-9_11

Staring, K., & Titlestad, O. (2006). Networks of open source health care action. *OSS*, *203*, 135–141.

Steinmacher, I., Silva, M. A. G., & Gerosa, M. A. (2014, May). Barriers Faced by Newcomers to Open Source Projects: A Systematic Review. In OSS (pp. 153-163). doi:10.1007/978-3-642-55128-4_21

Stol, K. J., Ali Babar, M., & Avgeriou, P. (2011). The importance of architectural knowledge in integrating open source software. *Open Source Systems: Grounding Research*, 142-158.

Stol, K. J., & Babar, M. A. (2009, June). Reporting empirical research in open source software: the state of practice. In *IFIP International Conference on Open Source Systems* (pp. 156-169). Springer. doi:10.1007/978-3-642-02032-2_15

Stol, K. J., & Babar, M. A. (2010, May). A comparison framework for open source software evaluation methods. In *IFIP International Conference on Open Source Systems* (pp. 389-394). Springer. doi:10.1007/978-3-642-13244-5_36

Studer, M. (2007, June). Community structure, individual participation and the social construction of merit. In *IFIP International Conference on Open Source Systems* (pp. 161-172). Springer. doi:10.1007/978-0-387-72486-7_13

Taibi, D., Del Bianco, V., Carbonare, D., Lavazza, L., & Morasca, S. (2008). Towards The Evaluation of OSS Trustworthiness: Lessons Learned From The Observation of Relevant OSS Projects. *Open Source Development, Communities and Quality*, 389-395.

Taibi, D., Lavazza, L., & Morasca, S. (2007). OpenBQR: a framework for the assessment of OSS. *Open Source Development, Adoption and Innovation*, 173-186.

Terceiro, A., Rios, L. R., & Chavez, C. (2010, September). An empirical study on the structural complexity introduced by core and peripheral developers in free software projects. In *Software Engineering (SBES), 2010 Brazilian Symposium on* (pp. 21-29). IEEE. doi:10.1109/SBES.2010.26

Tiangco, F., Stockwell, A., Sapsford, J., Rainer, A., & Swanton, E. (2005). *Open-source software in an occupational health application: The case of Heales Medical Ltd*. Procs.

Toth, K. (2006). Experiences with open source software engineering tools. *IEEE Software*, *23*(6), 44–52. doi:10.1109/MS.2006.158

Van Antwerp, M., & Madey, G. R. (2010, May). *Open Source Software Developer and Project Networks*. OSS. doi:10.1007/978-3-642-13244-5_39

Ven, K., Van Nuffel, D., & Verelst, J. (2006). The introduction of OpenOffice. org in the Brussels Public Administration. *Open Source Systems*, 123-134.

Ven, K., & Verelst, J. (2006, June). The organizational adoption of open source server software by Belgian organizations. In *IFIP International Conference on Open Source Systems* (pp. 111-122). Springer. doi:10.1007/0-387-34226-5_11

Viseur, R. (2012). From open source software to open source hardware. *Open Source Systems: Long-Term Sustainability*, 286-291.

Von Krogh, G., & Von Hippel, E. (2006). The promise of research on open source software. *Management Science*, *52*(7), 975–983. doi:10.1287/mnsc.1060.0560

Wasserman, A. I., Pal, M., & Chan, C. (2006). *The business readiness rating: a framework for evaluating open source*. EFOSS-Evaluation Framework for Open Source Software.

Weber, S. (2004). *Open source software in developing economies*. Academic Press.

Weinberg, G. M. (1971). *The psychology of computer programming* (Vol. 932633420). New York: Van Nostrand Reinhold.

Weiss, M., Moroiu, G., & Zhao, P. (2006). Evolution of open source communities. *Open Source Systems*, 21-32.

West, J. (2003). How open is open enough? Melding proprietary and open source platform strategies. *Research Policy*, *32*(7), 1259–1285. doi:10.1016/S0048-7333(03)00052-0

Wikimedia Foundation, Inc. (2017, March 11). *R (programming language)*. Retrieved March 11, 2017, from https://en.wikipedia.org/wiki/R_%28programming_language%29

Yamauchi, Y., Yokozawa, M., Shinohara, T., & Ishida, T. (2000, December). Collaboration with Lean Media: how open-source software succeeds. In *Proceedings of the 2000 ACM conference on Computer supported cooperative work* (pp. 329-338). ACM. doi:10.1145/358916.359004

Zhai, Z., Kijewski-Correa, T., Kareem, A., Hachen, D., & Madey, G. (2012, September). Citizen Engineering: Evolving OSS Practices to Engineering Design and Analysis. In *IFIP International Conference on Open Source Systems* (pp. 61-77). Springer. doi:10.1007/978-3-642-33442-9_5

ADDITIONAL READING

Adina, B. (2012). The impact of formal qa practices on floss communities – the case of mozilla. In *Open Source Systems* (pp. 262–267). Long-Term Sustainability.

Adina, B. (2013). The emergence of quality assurance practices in free/libre open source software: A case study. In *Open Source Software* (pp. 271–276). Quality Verification.

Amir, A., & Carlos, J. (2014). Drawing the big picture: Temporal visualization of dynamic collaboration graphs of oss software forks. In *Open Source Software* (pp. 41–50). Mobile Open Source Technologies.

Amir, H. M., & Mohammad, K. (2010). Bug localization using revision log analysis and open bug repository text categorization. In *Open Source Software* (pp. 188–199). New Horizons.

Amit, D., & Dirk, R. (2008). Continuous integration in open source software development. In *Open Source Development* (pp. 273–280). Communities and Quality.

Anders, S., Gabriela, A., Anne, S., & Daniel, K. S. (2007). Sprint-driven development: working, learning and the process of encultur- ation in the pypy community. In *Open Source Development* (pp. 133–146). Adoption and Innovation.

Andrea, B., & Cristina, R. (2005). Open source software, intrinsic mo- tivations and profit-oriented firms.do not firms practise what they preach? *Proceedings of the First International Conference on Open Source Systems.*

Andrea, C. (2009). Domain drivers in the modularization of floss systems. In *Open Source Ecosystems* (pp. 3–19). Diverse Communities Interacting.

Andrea, C., Cornelia, B., & Klaas-Jan, S. (2011). Successful reuse of software components: A report from the open source perspective. In *Open Source Systems* (pp. 159–176). Grounding Research.

Andrea, C., & Thomas, K. (2009). Software engineering in practice: Design and architectures of floss systems. In *Open Source Ecosystems* (pp. 34–46). Diverse Communities Interacting.

Andrea, J., Danila, P., Alberto, S., & Giancarlo, S. (2013). How to calculate software metrics for multiple languages using open source parsers. In *Open Source Software* (pp. 264–270). Quality Verification.

Anh, N. D., Daniela, S. C., Claudia, A., & Reidar, C. (2011). Impact of stakeholder type and collaboration on issue resolution time in foss projects. In *Open Source Systems* (pp. 1–16). Grounding Research.

Antikainen, M., Aaltonen, T., & Vaisanen, J. (2007). The role of trust in oss communitiescase linux kernel community. In *Open Source Development* (pp. 223–228). Adoption and Innovation.

Ayala, C., Hauge, Ø., Conradi, R., Franch, X., Li, J., & Velle, K. S. (2009). Challenges of the open source component mar- ketplace in the industry. In *Open Source Ecosystems* (pp. 213–224). Diverse Communities Interacting.

Ayala, C., Søensen, C.-F., Conradi, R., Franch, X., & Li, J. (2007). Open source collaboration for fostering off-the-shelf components selection. In *Open Source Development* (pp. 17–30). Adoption and Innovation. doi:10.1007/978-0-387-72486-7_2

Banzi, M., Bruno, G., & Caire, G. (2008). To what extent does it pay to approach open source software for a big telco player? In *Open Source Development* (pp. 307–315). Communities and Quality. doi:10.1007/978-0-387-09684-1_27

Bergquist, M., Ljungberg, J., & Rolandsson, B. (2011). A historical ac- count of the value of free and open source software: From software commune to commercial commons. In *Open Source Systems* (pp. 196–207). Grounding Research.

Boccacci, P., Carrega, V., & Dodero, G. (2007). Open source technologies for visually impaired people. In *Open Source Development* (pp. 241–246). Adoption and Innovation. doi:10.1007/978-0-387-72486-7_22

Boldyreff, C., Capiluppi, A., Knowles, T., & Munro, J. (2009). Undergraduate research opportunities in oss. In *Open Source Ecosystems* (pp. 340–350). Diverse Communities Interacting.

Bruno, R., Barbara, R., & Giancarlo, S. (2009). Analysis of open source software development iterations by means of burst detection techniques. In *Open Source Ecosystems* (pp. 83–93). Diverse Communities Interacting.

Bruno, R., Barbara, R., & Giancarlo, S. (2010a). Modelling failures occurrences of open source software with reliability growth. In *Open Source Software* (pp. 268–280). New Horizons.

Bruno, R., Barbara, R., & Giancarlo, S. (2010b). Download patterns and releases in open source software projects: A perfect symbiosis? In *Open Source Software* (pp. 252–267). New Horizons.

Cabano, M., Monti, C., & Piancastelli, G. (2007). Context-dependent evaluation methodology for open source software. In *Open Source Develop- ment* (pp. 301–306). Adoption and Innovation. doi:10.1007/978-0-387-72486-7_32

Capiluppi, A., Stol, K.-J., & Boldyreff, C. (2012). Exploring the role of commercial stakeholders in open source software evolution. In *Open Source Systems* (pp. 178–200). Long-Term Sustainability. doi:10.1007/978-3-642-33442-9_12

Capra, E., Francalanci, C., Merlo, F., & Lamastra, C. R. (2012). A survey on firms participation in open source community projects. In *Open Source Ecosystems* (pp. 225–236). Diverse Communities Interacting.

Celeste, L. P. (2009). A survey of usability practices in free/libre/open source software. In *Open Source Ecosystems* (pp. 264–273). Diverse Communities Interacting.

Chiara, F., & Francesco, M. (2008). Empirical analysis of the bug fixing process in open source projects. In *Open Source Development* (pp. 187–196). Communities and Quality.

Chintan, A., & Jos Van, H. (2010). Coordination implications of software coupling in open source projects. In *Open Source Software* (pp. 314–321). New Horizons.

Chris, J., & Walt, S. (2011). License update and migration processes in open source software projects. In *Open Source Systems* (pp. 177–195). Grounding Research.

Christopher, O. (2010). Introducing automated unit testing into open source projects. In *Open Source Software* (pp. 361–366). New Horizons.

Claudia, R., & William, R. (2011). Towards a unified definition of open source quality. In *Open Source Systems* (pp. 17–33). Grounding Research.

Claudio, A., Ernesto, D., Nabil, I., Fulvio, F., Pietro, G., & Romaric, T. (2008). Mapping linux security targets to existing test suites. In *Open Source Development* (pp. 29–45). Communities and Quality.

Conklin, M. (2007). Project entity matching across floss repositories. In *Open Source Development* (pp. 45–57). Adoption and Innovation.

Corbiere, A. (2008). A framework to abstract the design practices of e-learning system projects. In *Open Source Development* (pp. 317–323). Communities and Quality. doi:10.1007/978-0-387-09684-1_28

Dang, Q. V., Berger, O., Bac, C., & Hamet, B^. (2007). Authenticating from multiple authentication sources in a collaborative platform. In *Open Source Development* (pp. 229–234). Adoption and Innovation.

Daniel, I., Gregorio, R., & Jesu's, M. G. (2012). Do more experienced developers introduce fewer bugs? In *Open Source Systems* (pp. 268–273). Long-Term Sustainability.

Daniel, M. G., & Jesu's, M. G. (2009). An empirical study of the reuse of software licensed under the gnu general public license. In *Open Source Ecosystems* (pp. 185–198). Diverse Communities Interacting.

Darren, S. (2007). Stakeholder value, usage, needs and obligations from differnet types of f/loss licenses. In *Open Source Development* (pp. 343–348). Adoption and Innovation.

Del Bianco, V., Lavazza, L., Lenarduzzi, V., Morasca, S., Taibi, D., & Tosi, D. (2012). A study on oss marketing and communication strategies. In *Open Source Systems* (pp. 338–343). Long-Term Sustainability. doi:10.1007/978-3-642-33442-9_31

den Besten, M., & Dalle, J.-M. (2011). Something of a potemkin village? acid2 and mozillas efforts to comply with html4. In *Open Source Systems* (pp. 320–324). Grounding Research.

Di Cerbo, F., Dodero, G., & Succi, G. (2008). Social networking technologies for free-open source e-learning systems. In *Open Source Development* (pp. 289–297). Communities and Quality. doi:10.1007/978-0-387-09684-1_25

Dobusch, L. (2008). Migration discourse structures: Escaping Microsofts desktop path. In *Open Source Development* (pp. 223–235). Communities and Quality. doi:10.1007/978-0-387-09684-1_18

Durand, D., Vuattoux, J.-L., & Ditscheid, P.-J. (2012). Oss in 2012: A long-term sustainable alternative for corporate it. In *Open Source Sys- tems*. Long-Term Sustainability. doi:10.1007/978-3-642-33442-9_37

El Ioini, N., Garibbo, A., Sillitti, A., & Succi, G. (2013). An open source monitoring framework for enterprise soa. In *Open Source Software* (pp. 182–193). Quality Verification. doi:10.1007/978-3-642-38928-3_13

Etiel, P., Alberto, S., & Giancarlo, S. (2010). Comparing openbrr, qsos, and omm assessment models. In *Open Source Software* (pp. 224–238). New Horizons.

Fernandez-Ramil, J., Izquierdo-Cortazar, D., & Mens, T. (2009). What does it take to develop a million lines of open source code? In *Open Source Ecosystems* (pp. 170–184). Diverse Communities Interacting. doi:10.1007/978-3-642-02032-2_16

Fl'avia, L. A., & Fernanda, M. P. F. (2011). Aspects of an open source software sustainable life cycle. In *Open Source Systems* (pp. 325–329). Grounding Research.

Gamalielsson, J., Lundell, B., Grahn, A., Andersson, S., Feist, J., Gustavsson, T., & Strindberg, H. (2013). Towards a reference model on how to utilise open standards in open source projects: Experiences based on drupal. In *Open Source Software* (pp. 257–263). Quality Verification. doi:10.1007/978-3-642-38928-3_19

Gamalielsson, J., Lundell, B., & Lings, B. (2010). The nagios commu- nity: An extended quantitative analysis. In *Open Source Software* (pp. 85–96). New Horizons.

Gamalielsson, J., Lundell, B., & Mattsson, A. (2011). Open source software for model driven development: A case study. In *Open Source Systems* (pp. 348–367). Grounding Research. doi:10.1007/978-3-642-24418-6_30

Gao, Y., & Madey, G. (2007). Network analysis of the sourceforge. net community. In *Open Source Development* (pp. 187–200). Adoption and Innovation.

Giacalone, P. (2005). Oss implementation solutions for public administration applications. *Proceedings of the First International Conference on Open Source Systems*, 259–262.

Giuditta, D. P., & Dimitri, G. (2005). Proprietary software and open source philosophy: A shift in softwares production methods. *Proceedings of the First International Conference on Open Source Systems*.

Gottfried, H., Dirk, R., Carsten, K., & Wolfgang, M. (2013). A dual model of open source license growth. In *Open Source Software* (pp. 245–256). Quality Verification.

Gregorio, R., & Jesu's, M. G. (2012). A comprehensive study of software forks: Dates, reasons and outcomes. In *Open Source Systems* (pp. 1–14). Long-Term Sustainability.

Gunes, K., Dongsong, Z., & Hongfang, L. (2007). Effect of coupling on defect proneness in evolutionary open-source software development. In *Open Source Development* (pp. 271–276). Adoption and Innovation.

Gutsche, J. (2005). Competition between open source and proprietary software, and the scope for public policy. *International Conference on Open Source Systems*.

H'ela, M., den Besten, M., De Loupy, C., & Dalle, J.-M. (2009). Peeling the onion. In *Open Source Ecosystems* (pp. 284–297). Diverse Communities Interacting.

Hannemann, A., Liiva, K., & Klamma, R. (2014). Navigation support in evolving open-source communities by a web-based dashboard. In *Open Source Software* (pp. 11–20). Mobile Open Source Technologies. doi:10.1007/978-3-642-55128-4_2

Henttonen, K. (2011). Libre software as an innovation enabler in India experiences of a bangalorian software sme. In *Open Source Systems* (pp. 220–232). Grounding Research. doi:10.1007/978-3-642-24418-6_15

Howison, J., Wiggins, A., & Crowston, K. (2008). Research workflows for studying free and open source software development. In *Open Source Development* (pp. 405–411). Communities and Quality.

Iftekhar, A., Soroush, G., & Carlos, J. (2014). An exploration of code quality in foss projects. In *Open Source Software* (pp. 181–190). Mobile Open Source Technologies.

Iio, J., Shimizu, H., Sasaki, H., & Matsumoto, A. (2010). Pro- posal for solving incompatibility problems between open-source and pro- prietary web browsers. In *Open Source Software* (pp. 330–335). New Horizons.

Iv'an, A. V., Ceden~o, A. C., Joaqu'ın, C., & Gonza'lez, G. (2014). A performance analysis of wireless mesh networks implemen- tations based on open source software. In *Open Source Software* (pp. 107–110). Mobile Open Source Technologies.

Janczukowicz, E., Bouabdallah, A., Braud, A., Fromentoux, G., & Bonnin, J.-M. (2014). Improving mozillas in-app payment platform. In *Open Source Software* (pp. 103–106). Mobile Open Source Technologies.

Jean-Michel, D., & Matthijs, B. (2007). Different bug fixing regimes? a preliminary case for superbugs. In *Open Source Development* (pp. 247–252). Adoption and Innovation.

Jean-Michel, D., Matthijs, B., & H'ela, M. (2008). Channeling firefox developers: Mom and dad arent happy yet. In *Open Source Development* (pp. 265–271). Communities and Quality.

Jermakovics, A., Sillitti, A., & Succi, G. (2013). Exploring collaboration networks in open-source projects. In *Open Source Software* (pp. 97–108). Quality Verification.

Jesu's, M. G., Daniel, I., Gregorio, R., & Mario, G. (2014). Code review analytics: Webkit as case study. In *Open Source Software* (pp. 1–10). Mobile Open Source Technologies.

John, N. (2007). Innovation in open source software development: A tale of two features. In *Open Source Development* (pp. 109–120). Adoption and Innovation.

John, T., Andre, G., Paulo, T., & Jeff, J. (2011). Package upgrade robustness: An analysis for gnu/linux§R package management systems. In *Open Source Systems* (pp. 299–306). Grounding Research.

Jonas, G., & Bjørn, L. (2012). Long-term sustainability of open source software communities beyond a fork: A case study of libreoffice. In *Open Source Systems* (pp. 29–47). Long-Term Sustainability.

Kamei, Y., Matsumoto, S., Maeshima, H., Onishi, Y., Ohira, M., & Ken-ichi, M. (2008). Analysis of coordination between developers and users in the apache community. In *Open Source Development* (pp. 81–92). Communities and Quality. doi:10.1007/978-0-387-09684-1_7

Khondhu, J., Capiluppi, A., & Stol, K.-J. (2013). Is it all lost? a study of inactive open source projects. In *Open Source Software* (pp. 61–79). Quality Verification. doi:10.1007/978-3-642-38928-3_5

Kim, S., Yoo, J., & Lee, M. (2012). Step-by-step strategies and case studies for embedded software companies to adapt to the foss ecosystem. In *Open Source Systems* (pp. 48–60). Long-Term Sustainability. doi:10.1007/978-3-642-33442-9_4

Klaas-Jan, S., & Muhammad Ali, B. (2010). A comparison framework for open source software evaluation methods. In *Open Source Software* (pp. 389–394). New Horizons.

Klaas-Jan, S., Muhammad Ali, B., & Paris, A. (2011). The importance of architectural knowledge in integrating open source software. In *Open Source Systems* (pp. 142–158). Grounding Research.

Koch, S. (2007). Exploring the effects of coordination and communication tools on the efficiency of open source projects using data envelopment analysis. In *Open Source Development* (pp. 97–108). Adoption and Innovation. doi:10.1007/978-0-387-72486-7_8

Krivoruchko, J. (2007). The use of open source software in enterprise distributed computing environments. In *Open Source Development* (pp. 277–282). Adoption and Innovation. doi:10.1007/978-0-387-72486-7_28

Kuechler, V., Gilbertson, C., & Jensen, C. (2012). Gender differences in early free and open source software joining process. In *Open Source Systems* (pp. 78–93). Long-Term Sustainability. doi:10.1007/978-3-642-33442-9_6

Kuechler, V., Jensen, C., & Bryant, D. (2013). Misconceptions and barriers to adoption of foss in the US energy industry. In *Open Source Software* (pp. 232–244). Quality Verification.

Kurunsaari, M. (2012). Future smart metering runs on open source–challenges and the guruxami project. In *Open Source Systems* (pp. 389–394). Long-Term Sustainability. doi:10.1007/978-3-642-33442-9_40

Laisn'e, J.-P., Lago, N., Kon, F., & Coca, P. (2010). A network of floss competence centres. In *Open Source Software* (pp. 348–353). New Horizons.

Lakka, S., Stamati, T., & Martakos, D. (2012). Does oss affect e-government growth? an econometric analysis on the impacting factors. In *Open Source Systems* (pp. 292–297). Long-Term Sustainability. doi:10.1007/978-3-642-33442-9_24

Landon, J. P., Alexander, C. M., Charles, D. K., & Eric, K. R. (2011). Cliff walls: An analysis of monolithic commits using latent dirich- let allocation. In *Open Source Systems* (pp. 282–298). Grounding Research.

Laura, A. R., Gregorio, R., & Jesu's, M. (2013). A preliminary analysis of localization in free software: How translations are performed. In *Open Source Software* (pp. 153–167). Quality Verification.

Len, B., Rick, K., & Ipek, O. (2011). Developing architectural documentation for the hadoop distributed file system. In *Open Source Systems* (pp. 50–61). Grounding Research.

Lewis, J. (2013). The role of microblogging in oss knowledge management. In *Open Source Software* (pp. 140–152). Quality Verification. doi:10.1007/978-3-642-38928-3_10

Lindman, J. (2007). Shared assumption concerning technical determination in apache web server developer community. In *Open Source Development* (pp. 283–288). Adoption and Innovation. doi:10.1007/978-0-387-72486-7_29

Lindman, J., Juutilainen, J.-P., & Rossi, M. (2009). Beyond the busi- ness model: Incentives for organizations to publish software source code. In *Open Source Ecosystems* (pp. 47–56). Diverse Communities Interacting.

Lindman, J., Rossi, M., & Marttiin, P. (2008). Applying open source development practices inside a company. In *Open Source Development* (pp. 381–387). Communities and Quality. doi:10.1007/978-0-387-09684-1_36

Linus, N., & Tommi, M. (2011). To fork or not to fork: Fork motivations in sourceforge projects. In *Open Source Systems* (pp. 259–268). Grounding Research.

Linus, N., Tommi, M., Juho, L., & Martin, F. (2012). Per- spectives on code forking and sustainability in open source software. In *Open Source Systems* (pp. 274–279). Long-Term Sustainability.

Lo'pez, D., de Pablos, C., & Santos, R. (2010). Profiling f/oss adoption modes: An interpretive approach. In *Open Source Software* (pp. 354–360). New Horizons. doi:10.1007/978-3-642-13244-5_31

Luis, C., Andrea, J., Tadas, R., Juri, S., & Je-lena, V. (2012). A novel application of open source technologies to measure agile software development process. In *Open Source Systems* (pp. 316–321). Long-Term Sustainability.

Lundell, B., Persson, A., & Lings, B. (2007). Learning through practical involvement in the oss ecosystem: Experiences from a master's assignment. In *Open Source Development* (pp. 289–294). Adoption and Innovation. doi:10.1007/978-0-387-72486-7_30

Mario, S., & Andrea, B. (2013). Information security and open source dual use security software: Trust paradox. In *Open Source Software* (pp. 194–206). Quality Verification.

Martin, M., Francis, H., & David, P. (2005). Quality practices and problems in free software projects. *Proceedings of the First International Conference on Open Source Systems*, 24–28.

Martin, M., Francis, H., & David, P. (2007). Release management in free software projects: Practices and problems. In *Open Source Development* (pp. 295–300). Adoption and Innovation.

Martinez, A. (2005). Open source, a development option. *Proceedings of the First International Conference on Open Source Systems*.

Matos, A., Thomson, J., & Trezentos, P. (2011). Preparing floss for future network paradigms: A survey on linux network management. In *Open Source Systems* (pp. 75–89). Grounding Research. doi:10.1007/978-3-642-24418-6_6

Matthias, S. (2007). Community structure, individual participation and the social construction of merit. In *Open Source Development* (pp. 161–172). Adoption and Innovation.

Mavridis, A., Fotakidis, D., & Stamelos, I. (2012). Open source migration in Greek public sector: A feasibility study. In *Open Source Systems* (pp. 233–243). Long-Term Sustainability. doi:10.1007/978-3-642-33442-9_15

Michael, J. S., Na, L., Robert, H., & Kevin, C. (2009). Group maintenance behaviors of core and peripherial members of free/libre open source software teams. In *Open Source Ecosystems* (pp. 298–309). Diverse Communities Interacting.

Morgan, L. (2005). An analysis of cospa a consortium for open source in the public administration. *First International Conference on Open Source Systems.*

Mulazzani, F., Rossi, B., Russo, B., & Steff, M. (2011). Building knowledge in open source software research in six years of conferences. In *Open Source Systems* (pp. 123–141). Grounding Research. doi:10.1007/978-3-642-24418-6_9

Netta, I. (2010). Usability innovations in oss development–examining user innovations in an oss usability discussion forum. In *Open Source Software* (pp. 119–129). New Horizons.

Netta, I., Henrik, H., & Tanja, K. (2008). Usability in company open source software context-initial findings from an empirical case study. In *Open Source Development* (pp. 359–365). Communities and Quality.

Noda, T., Tansho, T., & Coughlan, S. (2011). Standing situations and issues of open source policy in East Asian nations: Outcomes of open source research workshop of East Asia. In *Open Source Systems* (pp. 379–384). Grounding Research. doi:10.1007/978-3-642-24418-6_32

Noda, T., Tansho, T., & Coughlan, S. (2013). Effect on business growth by utilization and contribution of open source software in Japanese it companies. In *Open Source Software* (pp. 222–231). Quality Verification. doi:10.1007/978-3-642-38928-3_16

Noll, J. (2009). What constitutes open source? a study of the vista electronic medical record software. In *Open Source Ecosystems* (pp. 310–319). Diverse Communities Interacting. doi:10.1007/978-3-642-02032-2_27

Noll, J., Seichter, D., & Beecham, S. (2012). A qualitative method for mining open source software repositories. In *Open Source Systems* (pp. 256–261). Long- Term Sustainability. doi:10.1007/978-3-642-33442-9_18

Olivier, B., & Christian, B. (2013). Authoritative linked data descriptions of debian source packages using adms. In *Open Source Software* (pp. 168–181). Quality Verification.

Orsila, H., Geldenhuys, J., Ruokonen, A., & Hammouda, I. (2008). Update propagation practices in highly reusable open source components. In *Open Source Development* (pp. 159–170). Communities and Quality. doi:10.1007/978-0-387-09684-1_13

Ozel, B., Jovanovic, U., Oba, B., & van Leeuwen, M. (2007). Perceptions on f/oss adoption. In *Open Source Development* (pp. 319–324). Adoption and Innovation.

Paolo, C. (2010). To patent or not to patent: a pilot experiment on incentives to copyright in a sequential innovation setting. In *Open Source Software* (pp. 53–72). New Horizons.

Paul, J. A., Andrea, C., & Adriaan, G. (2008). Detecting agility of open source projects through developer engagement. In *Open Source Development* (pp. 333–341). Communities and Quality.

Paula, M. B., & John, M. C. (2009). Floss ux design: An analysis of user experience design in firefox and openoffice. org. In *Open Source Ecosystems* (pp. 237–250). Diverse Communities Interacting.

Petrinja, E., Sillitti, A., & Succi, G. (2008). Overview on trust in large floss communities. In *Open Source Development* (pp. 47–56). Communities and Quality. doi:10.1007/978-0-387-09684-1_4

Petrinja, E., Sillitti, A., & Succi, G. (2011). Adoption of oss development practices by the software industry: A survey. In *Open Source Systems* (pp. 233–243). Grounding Research. doi:10.1007/978-3-642-24418-6_16

Philipp, H., & Dirk, R. (2009). Estimating commit sizes efficiently. In *Open Source Ecosystems* (pp. 105–115). Diverse Communities Interacting.

Quinn, C. T., Jonathan, L. K., Alexander, C. M., & Charles, D. K. (2011). An analysis of author contribution patterns in eclipse foundation project source code. In *Open Source Systems* (pp. 269–281). Grounding Research.

Rainer, A., & Gale, S. (2005). Evaluating the quality and quantity of data on open source software projects. *Procs 1st Int Conf on Open Source Software*.

Rantalainen, A., Hedberg, H., & Iivari, N. (2011). A review of tool support for user-related communication in floss development. In *Open Source Systems* (pp. 90–105). Grounding Research. doi:10.1007/978-3-642-24418-6_7

Richard, T., Robert, F., & Tony, G. (2008). Extracting generally applicable patterns from object-oriented programs for the purpose of test case creation. In *Open Source Development* (pp. 281–287). Communities and Quality.

Rosales Rosa, E., Alfonso F'ırvida Don'estevez, A., Gonz'alez Mun˜o, M., & Pierra Fuentes, A. (2014). Smart tv with free technologies in support of teaching-learning process. In *Open Source Software* (pp. 147–152). Mobile Open Source Technologies. doi:10.1007/978-3-642-55128-4_20

Rosales Rosa, E., Manuel Fuentes Rodr'ıguez, J., Alfonso F'ırvida Don'estevez, A., & Garc'ıa Rivas, D. (2014). Cuban gnu/linux nova distribution for server computers. In *Open Source Software* (pp. 212–215). Mobile Open Source Technologies. doi:10.1007/978-3-642-55128-4_31

Rossi, B., Russo, B., & Succi, G. (2007). Open source software and open data standards as a form of technology adoption: a case study. In *Open Source Development* (pp. 325–330). Adoption and Innovation. doi:10.1007/978-0-387-72486-7_36

Scacchi, W. (2011). Modding as an open source approach to extending computer game systems. In *Open Source Systems* (pp. 62–74). Grounding Research. doi:10.1007/978-3-642-24418-6_5

Stefan, K., & Volker, S. (2008). Open source project categorization based on growth rate analysis and portfolio planning methods. In *Open Source Development* (pp. 375–380). Communities and Quality.

Steinmacher, I., Aur'elio Graciotto Silva, M., & Aur'elio Gerosa, M. (2014). Barriers faced by newcomers to open source projects: a systematic review. In *Open Source Software* (pp. 153–163). Mobile Open Source Technologies. doi:10.1007/978-3-642-55128-4_21

Taibi, D., Del Bianco, V., Carbonare, D. D., Lavazza, L., & Morasca, S. (2008). Towards the evaluation of oss trustworthiness: Lessons learned from the observation of relevant oss projects. In *Open Source De- velopment* (pp. 389–395). Communities and Quality. doi:10.1007/978-0-387-09684-1_37

Tetsuo, N., Terutaka, T., & Shane, C. (2012). The effect of open source licensing on the evolution of business strategy. In *Open Source Systems* (pp. 344–349). Long-Term Sustainability.

Tiangco, F., Stockwell, A., Sapsford, J., Rainer, A., & Swanton, E. (2005). Open-source software in an occupational health application: the case of heales medical ltd. *Procs 1st Int Conf on Open Source Software*.

Vieri, D. B., Luigi, L., Sandro, M., & Davide, T. (2009). Quality of open source software: The qualipso trustworthiness model. In *Open Source Ecosystems* (pp. 199–212). Diverse Communities Interacting.

Vieri, D. B., Luigi, L., Sandro, M., Davide, T., & Davide, T. (2010). An investigation of the user's perception of oss quality. In *Open Source Software* (pp. 15–28). New Horizons.

Vincenzo, D., Stefano, D. P., & Maurizio, T. (2008). Open to grok. how do hackers practices produce hackers? In *Open Source Development* (pp. 121–129). Communities and Quality.

Viseur, R. (2012). From open source software to open source hardware. In *Open Source Systems* (pp. 286–291). Long-Term Sustainability. doi:10.1007/978-3-642-33442-9_23

Viseur, R. (2013). Identifying success factors for the mozilla project. In *Open Source Software* (pp. 45–60). Quality Verification. doi:10.1007/978-3-642-38928-3_4

Wiggins, A., Howison, J., & Crowston, K. (2008). Social dynamics of floss team communication across channels. In *Open Source Development* (pp. 131–142). Communities and Quality. doi:10.1007/978-0-387-09684-1_11

Xavier, F., Ron, K., Fabio, M., Angelo, S., David, A., Ron, B., & Alberto, S. (2014). A layered approach to managing risks in oss projects. In *Open Source Software* (pp. 168–171). Mobile Open Source Technologies.

Yamakami, T. (2010). Challenges for mobile middleware platform: issues for embedded open source software integration. In *Open Source Software* (pp. 401–406). New Horizons. doi:10.1007/978-3-642-13244-5_38

Yamakami, T. (2010). An exploratory long-term open source activity analysis: Implications from empirical findings on activity statistics. In *Open Source Software* (pp. 395–400). New Horizons. doi:10.1007/978-3-642-13244-5_37

Yamakami, T. (2011). The third generation of oss: A three-stage evolu- tion from gift to commerce-economy. In *Open Source Systems* (pp. 368–378). Grounding Research. doi:10.1007/978-3-642-24418-6_31

Chapter 2
Macro Studies of FOSS Ecology

ABSTRACT

The ecology of Free and Open Source Software (FOSS) is dotted by projects of every kind ranging from small desktop applications to large mission critical systems. To enable maximum visibility among the developer community, these projects are often hosted in community project management portals. The current work studies one such portal, sourceforge.net by analyzing the data of 200,000 projects and 2 million developers for the period Feb 2005 to Aug 2009. The scope of the present study includes the analysis of developer contribution. The slow growth rate of developer community and high number of single developer projects are the major findings of the present work.

INTRODUCTION

Traditional software development has been characterized by the strict organization of developer teams. Almost all formal methodologies insist on layered structure of developers with responsibilities clearly delineated. The decision-making powers are vested with the few who control huge army of developers. There are established rules on when people can be added or dropped from a project. Informal observations like the one done by Fredrick Brooks "adding manpower to a late software project makes it late" (Brooks, 1995) have been accepted as law. In other words, the priestly order followed in software development makes the whole system impenetrable by outsiders.

DOI: 10.4018/978-1-5225-3707-6.ch002

On the contrary, the FOSS development methods seldom follow a closed-door policy towards developers. The system here thrives on the contribution of volunteers. Unsolicited cooperation between developers scattered across the globe, communicating with each other using digital media is the characteristic feature of FOSS development.

There are questions on the extent to which people are using this opportunity to be a part of software development. Contributing to software development requires certain technical competence. To expect technically trained developers to contribute to projects which are not part of their work and which does not benefit them monetarily is difficult.

Recent research has shown that people do contribute to FOSS for a variety of reasons. But the exact number of people involved in the development of FOSS is not clear. The difficulty arises from the fact that though there are number of websites like sourceforge.net which hosts thousands of FOSS projects there are equal number of projects hosted in their own dedicated sites. To collect the data from all these diverse sources is extremely difficult. Therefore, the data only from Sourceforge.net is considered for present studies.

PROCEDURE

Sourceforge.net maintains the data in a relational database. To extract the developer count from this dataset the relation USER GROUP is selected. The structure of the relation is given in Table 1.

The attribute USER ID is used to count the number of developers for each month and GROUP ID is used for counting the projects. The process for counting developers and projects for all months is given below

$S \leftarrow \{S_1, S_2 ... S_{52}\}$ original datasets

$A_i \leftarrow \varphi(X), \forall X \in S$ select unique developers

$A \leftarrow \{A_1, A_2 ... A_{52}\}$

$Bi \leftarrow \psi(X), \forall X \in S$ select unique projects

$B \leftarrow \{B_1, B_2 ... B_{52}\}$

$x_i \leftarrow |C|, \forall C \in A$ count the developers

$y_i \leftarrow |C|, \forall C \in B$ count the projects

$D \leftarrow \{x_1, x_2, ..., x_{52}\}$ list of developer count

$P \leftarrow \{y_1, y_2, ..., y_{52}\}$ list of project count

Using the relation USER GROUP we can also extract the number of developers subscribing to each project. The procedure for doing this activity is mentioned below

$S \leftarrow \{S_1, S_2 ... S_{52}\}$ original datasets

$A \leftarrow \varphi(X), X \in S$ select unique developers

$B \leftarrow \psi(X), X \in S$ select unique projects

$C \leftarrow \{x, |x \in A, y \in B, x \rightarrow y\}$

RESULTS AND DISCUSSION

The growth pattern of developers and projects in Sourceforge.net is summarized in Figure 1. The number of developers and projects are significant metrics since it can be used to gauge the interest among the general public to participate in FOSS development. The number of developers (Developer count) for all 54 datasets is given in Figure 2. The number of projects (Project count) in these time period is in Figure 3.

The statistical summary of the Developer count is given in Table 2. The statistical summary of the Project count is given in Table 3

Sourceforge.net in its website (as on Sep 2009) claims that it has 2 million registered users. But the result from this work shows that the maximum number of developers for any month is 246119. Therefore, it clears that only 10% of the registered users in sourceforge.net actually subscribe themselves to projects.

Table 1. Structure of table USER_GROUP

Column	Type	Modifiers
user group id	integer	not null
user id	integer	not null default 0
group id	integer	not null default 0
admin flags	character(16)	not null default ''::bpchar
forum flags	integer	not null default 0
project flags	integer	not null default 2
doc flags	integer	not null default 0
member role	integer	not null default 100
release flags	integer	not null default 0
artifact flags	integer	not null default 0
added by	integer	not null default 100
grantcvs	integer	not null default 1
grantshell	integer	not null default 1
row modtime	integer	not null
news flags	integer	not null default 0
screenshotflags	integer	not null default 0
grantsvn	integer	not null default 1

Table 2. Summary statistics of developer count

Mean	Median	Minimum	Maximum
194492.	200406.	83120.0	246119.
Std. Dev.	C.V.	Skewness	Ex. kurtosis
33139.3	0.170389	−0.922382	1.01698

Table 3. Summary statistics of project count

Mean	Median	Minimum	Maximum
149647.	152972.	65082.0	187512.
Std. Dev.	C.V.	Skewness	Ex. kurtosis
26278.5	0.175603	−1.0541	1.14948

Table 4. Frequency distribution of developers in Aug09 (complete)

Interval	Frequency	Relative %
≤14	159043	99.10%
14 - 28	1107	0.69%
28 - 42	188	0.12%
42 - 56	68	0.04%
56 - 70	33	0.02%
70 - 84	18	0.01%

Table 5. Frequency distribution of developers in Aug09 (up to 10 developers/project)

Number of Developers	Frequency	Relative %
1	111625	69.56%
2	23332	14.54%
3	9650	6.01%
4	5214	3.25%
5	3131	1.95%
6	1954	1.22%
7	1242	0.77%
8	902	0.56%
9	639	0.40%
10	470	0.29%

The number of developers in a given project is a important indicator of the popularity of a project. This measure can also be used to study the pattern of team organization in FOSS projects. By applying the method defined in the previous section, the number of developers subscribing to project for the data set of Aug09 is calculated. The result obtained is given in Table 4. This shows an important trend that more than 99% of the projects have less than 14 developers. This data is further analyzed to find the extent of distribution of developers in projects. The result is summarized in Table 5 which clearly shows that nearly 70% of the projects have only one developer.

This process is carried out for all 54 datasets. The result obtained is given in Figure 4. This clearly shows that on an average in every month 71% of the projects have only one developer.

Figure 1. Developers and projects in Sourceforge.net

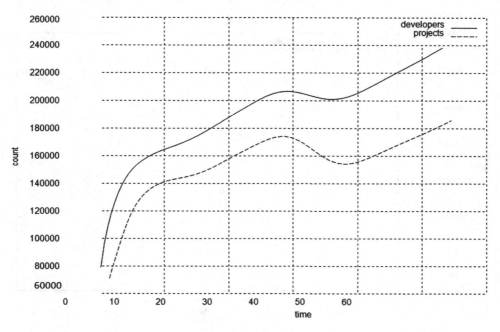

Figure 2. Developer count in Sourceforge.net

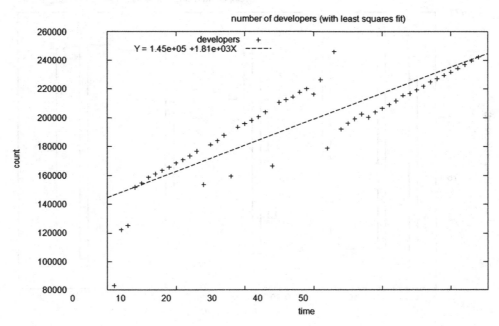

Figure 3. Project count in Sourceforge.net

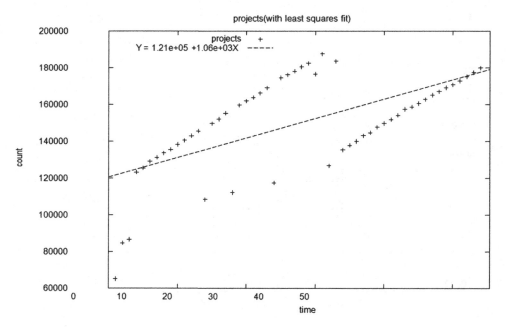

Figure 4. Developers with single project

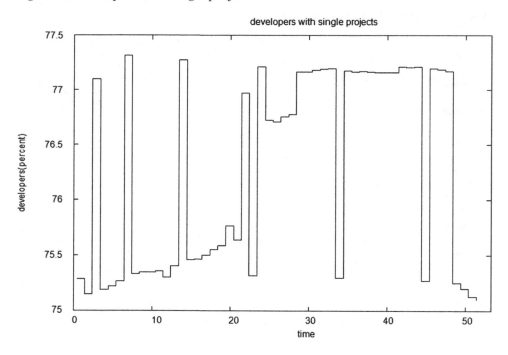

The number of projects subscribed by a developer is also an interesting metric. It shows the involvement of a development in FOSS development. If the developer has subscribed to a single project, it can be assumed that he is completely committed to that project.

The process of finding out the number of developers who subscribe to single project is carried out for all 54 datasets. The result obtained is given in Figure 5. This clearly shows that nearly 76% of developers subscribe to single project.

Figure 5. Projects with single developer

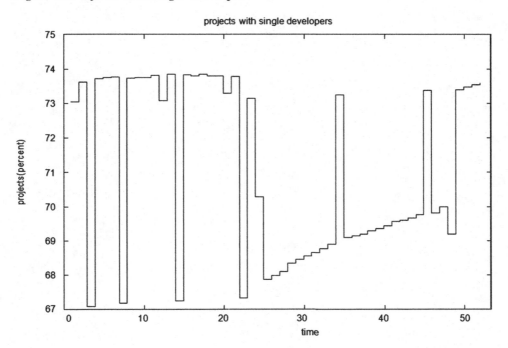

CONCLUSION

The analysis of the datasets from Feb 2005 to Aug 2009 yields following results

1. Only 10% of the Registered users in Sourceforge.net subscribe themselves to a Project
2. The average number of Developers is 200000
3. The average number of Projects is150000
4. 99% of Projects have less than 14 Developers
5. 71% of the Projects have single Developers
6. 76% of the Developers subscribe to only one Project

REFERENCES

Brooks, F.P. (1995). *The Mythical Man-Month: Essays on Software Engineering*. Addison-Wesley Professional.

Chapter 3
Micro Studies of FOSS Ecology

ABSTRACT

Sourceforge.net is the largest portal hosting Free and Open Source Software (FOSS). Among the projects available in sourceforge.net, six top ranked projects are selected for studying global volunteer collaboration patterns over a period of 6 years (2005-2011). It is found that a small set of volunteers do most of the work in these projects. The growth rate of volunteers, identification of core developers, join and drop rate of volunteers, task allocation and rate of task completion, movement of existing volunteers among different projects and the rate of new volunteer inclusion are also studied.

INTRODUCTION

The macro studies discussed the essential characteristics of the FOSS ecology. The size and nature of the projects and developers involved in FOSS development in a large project eco-system like Sourceforge.net were discussed. But the studies were limited in their scope. The important metrics like number of developers working on each project, their movement in the ecology, number of tasks which come up in projects and how effectively they are completed cannot be studied for all 150,000 projects. Therefore, it becomes necessary to study the important features of FOSS development by selecting few projects and subjecting them to rigorousanalysis.

DOI: 10.4018/978-1-5225-3707-6.ch003

Selection of Projects for Micro Analysis

To select few projects from a large pool of projects currently active in Sourceforge.net, the following options were available

1. Randomly choose few sampleprojects
2. Select one project from eachyear
3. Select projects which meets certain criteria

Random selection was rejected because the intention of the current study is to rigorously analyse the projects to detect common pattern among them. Choosing a project from every year would be beneficial if the focus of studies was time-series analysis of the evolution of FOSS. Therefore, the appropriate method is to select those projects which meet certain identified criteria.

The requirement for such a study would be to select those projects who have been proved successful. In traditional software world, quantifying success is easy because there are metrics such as number of sales. But in FOSS ecology such a metric loses its significance. Therefore, it was decided to use a metric identified by the Sourceforge.net as the measure of success.

Table 1. Structure of table STATS GROUP_RANK_BYMONTH

Column	Type	Modifiers
group id	integer	not null default 0
rankdate	integer	not null default 0
ranking	integer	not null default 0
percentile	double precision	default 0.0
score	bigint	not null default(0)::bigint

Table 2. Top ranked projects inSourceforge.net

Project-Id	Name
1	SourceForge.net
235	Pidgin
84122	Azureus
162271	Openbravo ERP
176962	ADempiere ERP Business Suite
196195	PostBooks ERP

Sourceforge.net has the practice of ranking all the projects hosted in its sitebased on a fixed formula. This data is captured in the table STATS_ GROUP_RANK_BYMONTH. The structure of this table is given in Table 1.

The projects which have remained in top position (Rank 1) for more than two consecutive months were selected as candidates for further analysis. The list of selected projects is given in Table 2

Growth Pattern of Developers

The surest sign of the success of a FOSS project is the increase in the number of developers working on that project. The attractiveness of FOSS projects is that anyone who is interested can become a stakeholder in the development of the software. The projects are open to all and there are no restrictions imposed on a developer once he joins a particular project. Given the perception about the success of the FOSS projects it is natural to assume that the number of developers in top projects keep increasing over time.

The procedure followed for finding the number of developers for a given project over the time period is given below:

```
Let P be the Project under study
Let (x,y) be an entry in Project_Develop[i]
if y subscribes to project x for the month i
Let D[i] be the number of Developers subscribed to P in the
month i
FOR i in (1 to 52)
DO
x:=P
D[i]:=COUNT(PROJECT_DEVELOP[x][y])
DONE
```

The result obtained by appying the above procedure to find the number of developers for the top projects from Feb 2005 to Aug 2008 is given in Figure 1 and Figure 2.

It can be observed that there is a steady increase in the number of developers subscribing to the top projects indicating the growing interest in those projects.

Developer Dedication

The previous discussion proved that there is a growing interest among developers to join top projects demonstrated through the increasing number of subscriber. But the question of how serious the developers are remains

Figure 1. Developer Growth: 1

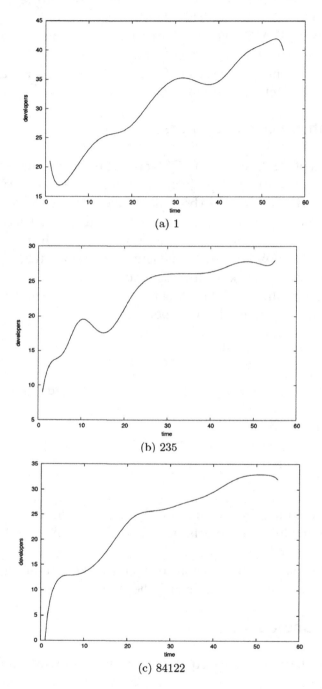

(a) 1

(b) 235

(c) 84122

Figure 2. Developer Growth: 2

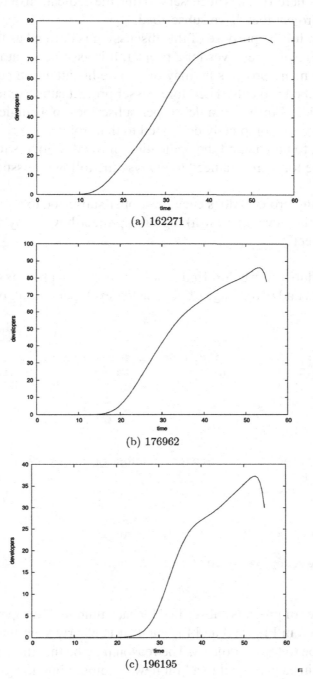

(a) 162271

(b) 176962

(c) 196195

unanswered. Therefore, it is necessary to find the dedication of the developers towards the project they have subscribed.

Dedication for the purpose of this discussion is defined as the amount of attention a developer reserves for a project. It is assumed that if a developer subscribes to many projects he may distribute his attention equally among all the subscribed projects. Therefore, lesser project subscription will imply more dedication. Further, if a developer subscribes to a single project, it is assumed that he is completely dedicated to thatproject.

Therefore, to understand the dedication of the developers to the projects they subscribe to, there is a need to analyse the following issues

- How many projects does each developer subscribe to?
- Among the developers working on a project how many work only on that project?

The procedure given below finds both the number of projects subscribed by the developers and percentage of dedicated developers for a given project P.

```
FOR i IN (1 to 54)
DO
Dev_List[i]:= list of unique developers working in P for the
month i Tot_Dev[i]:=Count of unique developers working in P for
the month i DONE
FOR i IN (1 to 54)
DO
FOR j in Dev_List[i]
DO
Proj_Count[j]:=count of projects subscribed by each developer
DONE
x:= COUNT(Proj_Count)
FOR k IN (1 to x)
DO
IF (Proj_Count[k] = 1) Ded_Dvlp_Count[i]++
DONE
Dedicated_Developers:= (Ded_Dvlp_Count[i] / Tot_Dev[i]) * 100
DONE
```

The number of projects subscribed by each unique developer in every top project is given in Figure 3 and Figure 4. It is clearly seen that majority of them subscribe to fewer projects. The reason may be that there exists a strict protocol within each project to admit new developer into the group. Though anyone can theoretically subscribe to any project, the rights to committ and make important changes is limited to few.

Table 3. Dedicated developers in top projects

Project-Id	Dedicated Developers (Percent)
1	29
235	51
84122	83
162271	92
176962	76
196195	89
Average	70

The results of finding dedicated developers in top projects are listed in Table 3. It is observed that on an average 70% of the developers in these projects are dedicated developers. This means the success of these projects may be attributed to the dedication of large number ofdevelopers.

Developer Join and Drop Patterns

The previous discussion answered the question of how developers subscribe to top projects. But the discussion does not consider the actual movement of developers from and to the project under discussion. The use of summary data misses the actual data that needs to be studied.

The scenario is clearly defined in the following example:

```
let D[i] be the list of unique developers in project P for
month i
let D[j] be the list of unique developers in project P for
month i+1
assume,
D[i]:= {a, b, c, d, e}
D[j]:= {a, d, e, f, g, h}
```

The procedure defined earlier would have identified the difference in number of developers as 1. Though this is true, there is a drastic change in the composition of the developers in consecutive datasets. Since the changing patterns of developer subscription holds important clues for the behaviour in FOSS ecology, the study of such movements is undertaken here.

Continuing the example mentioned above,

Figure 3. Projects subscribed by Developers: 1

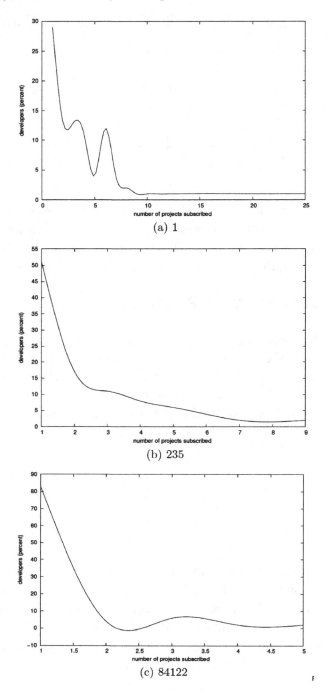

(a) 1

(b) 235

(c) 84122

Figure 4. Projects subscribed by developers: 2

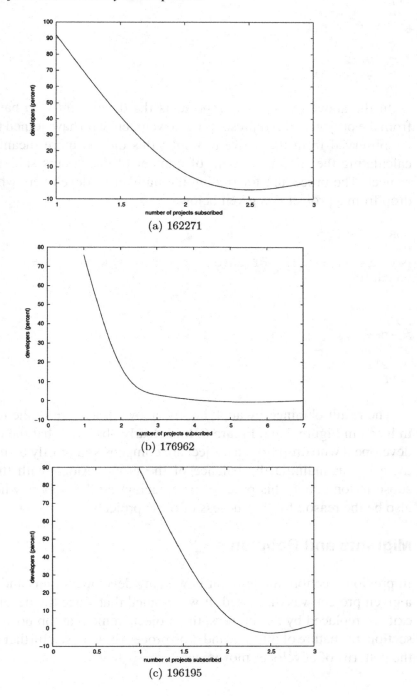

(a) 162271

(b) 176962

(c) 196195

```
if,
A = D[i] - D[j]
B = D[j] - D[i]
then,
A = {b, c}
B = {f, g, h}
```

In the above example, A represents the developers who have dropped from the project and B represents the developers who have joined the project. As observed from the above example, this data is more meaningful than calculating the summary count of number of developers subscribing to a project. The procedure for finding the number of developers who join and drop from a project P is given below

```
FOR i IN (1 to 54)
DO
Dev_List[i]:= list of unique developers working in P for the
month i
DONE
FOR i IN (1 to 53)
DO
A:=Dev_List[i] B:=Dev_List[i+1]
JOIN[i] = B - A
DROP[i] = A - B
DONE
```

The result obtained by applying the above procedure to the top projects in listed in Figure 5 and Figure 6. It is clearly observed that the numbers of developers who drop from a project are compensated mostly by new comers there by maintaining the balance of the group. Along with the growing subscription count, this process of replacing the developers who exit may also be the reason for the success of these projects.

Migrants and Debutants

In previous section, the issue of how many developers joins and drop from a given project was discussed. It was argued that since the developers who exit are replaced by newcomers, the projects remain at top position. In this section, the nature of this join and drop process is analysed further to discover the patterns of developer movement.

Figure 5. Developer join and drop patterns: 1

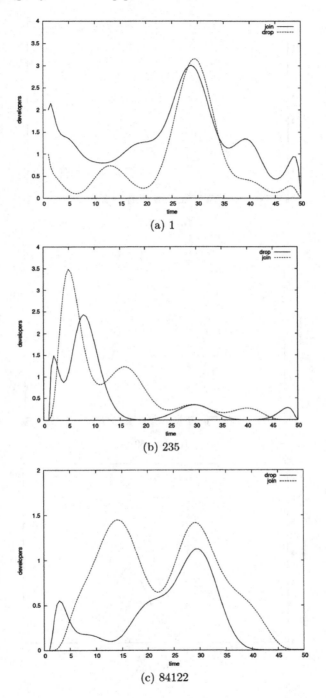

(a) 1

(b) 235

(c) 84122

Figure 6. Developer join and drop patterns: 2

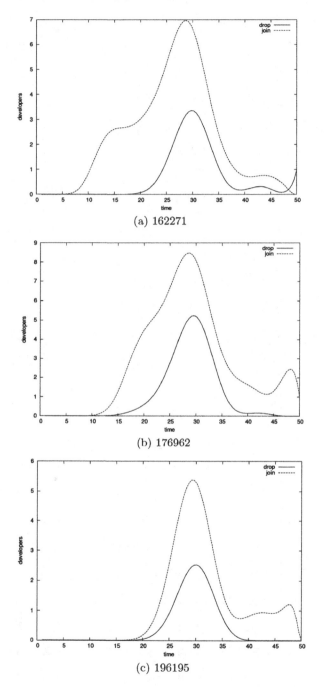

(a) 162271

(b) 176962

(c) 196195

One of the promises of FOSS development model is the open access for all interested people to join as developers. The success of the FOSS projects is often attributed to such massive participation of people. Eric Raymond has called this phenomenon as 'LinusLaw' which says: "Given enough eyeballs, all bugs are shallow…" Formally it is written as "Given a large enough beta-tester and co-developer base, almost every problem will be characterised quickly and the fix will be obvious to someone" (Raymond, 1999).

Therefore, it is clear that the celebrated factor of FOSS culture is open in- vitation to people to participate in projects. The previous section did try to answer this question. But the nature of developers who join the project remains unexplored. In this section, we undertake this activity by calculating the number of developers who migrate to a project from other projects and who start their journey in FOSS through one project.

For the rest of this section, the following definitions apply while referring to a project P in the month i.

- **MIGRANT:** A developer who has already subscribed to at-least one project other than P in months 1 to i-1
- **DEBUTANT:** A developer who has subscribed to only P in i and has not subscribed to any project in months 1 to i-1

The extent of migrants and debutants present in a project will clearly demon- strate the extent of applicability of important statements like Linus Law in FOSS ecology. The procedure for finding the migrants and debutants in project P is given below:

```
JOIN[i] is the list of developers who joined P in month i Dev_
List[i] is the list of unique developers of P in month i
FOR i IN (1 to 53)
DO
FOR j IN JOIN[i]
DO
FOR k in (1 to i-1)
DO
        IF (j IN Dev_List[k])
        DO
        Migrant[i]++ NEXT j
                DONE
         DONE
         Debutant[i]++
        DONE
DONE
```

Table 4. Migrants and debutants in top projects

Project-Id	Total Developers	Migrants	Debutants
1	68	37	31
235	35	17	18
84122	37	18	19
162271	114	32	82
176962	143	68	75
196195	61	29	32
Average	76	34	42

The result of applying this procedure to top projects is listed in Table 4. It is clearly seen that there is a equal measure of debutants and migrants in these projects. It clearly demonstrates that FOSS projects live up to their slogan of openness regarding membership to their projects. The average of 42% debutants proves this beyonddoubt.

CONCLUSION

The analysis of Six Top Ranked Projects from Feb 2005 to Aug 2009 yields following results

1. The average number of Developers is 76
2. 70% of the Developers are dedicated Developers
3. 34% of the Developers who join Top Projects migrate from other Projects (Migrants)
4. 42% of the Developers who join Top Projects are Newbie's (Debutants)

REFERENCES

Raymond, E. S. (1999). The Cathedral and the Bazaar. O'Reilly.

Chapter 4
Studies of Project Tasks

ABSTRACT

Among the projects available in sourceforge.net, the three top ranked projects are selected for studying the pattern of project tasks over a period of 6 years (2005-2011). It is found that the number of tasks in projects decrease with time in these projects. It is also observed that the amount of time taken to complete the task decrease with time. The developers alloted to tasks in a project, success rate the developers complete the tasks completely, and active contribution to the project by completing the alloted tasks of the volunteers are also studied.

INTRODUCTION

Software products are examples of complex systems. The complexity of software is due to the large number of requirements such a product should satisfy. Additionally, the development of software demands diverse skill sets, technically and other, which one person cannot possibly posses. Any software which is expected to run in real world is therefore built by a group of developers. This feature of software development has forced the practitioners to adopt some design principles to accommodate multiple developers working on a project.

DOI: 10.4018/978-1-5225-3707-6.ch004

The earliest attempt to solve this problem wasto divide the software development process into various related activities. All the process models and methodologies used in software engineering embody this idea. The basic activities of analysis, design, code, test and maintenance are common to all devel- opment methods. This separation of concern gives an opportunity to divide the software development into tasks which can be allotted to each individual developer or groups ofdevelopers.

Another way to solve the problem of synchronising multiple developers isfollowing the design principle of modularity. Modularity helps to isolate functional elements of the system. One module may be debugged, improved, or extended with minimal interaction to system discontinuity. As important as modularity is specification.

The key to production success of any modular construct is a rigid specification of the interfaces. They also help in the maintenance task by supplying the documentation necessary to train, understand, and provide maintenance.

The principles of separation of concern and modularity are applied extensively in development of FOSS. Modularising the software component allows parallelism and thus speeds up the process of development. Modularising also allows the developers to select a particular task to complete. In this chapter, the studies of such project tasks are undertaken. The number of tasks in each project, time taken for completing the tasks, the allocation of tasks to developers and the amount of tasks they complete are studied.

Number of Project Tasks

The activity in the FOSS project can be measured in different ways. The most definite metric is the number of commits made to the source code. But that does not capture the various other tasks undertaken by participants in the project. There are very broad set of activities that occur in a FOSS project like requesting new features, reporting bugs, support requests, documentation, localisation and internationalisation. To cover all the possible tasks that occur in a project, the Table PROJECT_TASK is used. The structure of this table is given in Table 1.

The procedure for finding the number of tasks in the project P is as follows

```
FOR i in (1 to 54)
DO
FOR ALL in Project_Task
```

Table 1. Structure of table PROJECT_TASK

Column	Type	Modifiers
project task id	integer	not null
group projectid	integer	not null default 0
summary	text	not null default ''::text
details	text	not null default ''::text
percent complete	integer	not null default 0
priority	integer	not null default 0
hours	double precision	not null default (0)::double precision
start date	integer	not null default 0
end date	integer	not null default 0
created by	integer	not null default 0
status id	integer	not null default 0

```
DO
IF (Project_Task[i].Project_Group_ID = P)
 P_Task[i]++
DONE
DONE
```

This procedure was applied only for three Top Ranked projects with the ids 184122 and 176962. The results are given in Figure 1. The results for other three Top Ranked projects were not significant. Hence, they were not considered for discussion. It is observed that the number of tasks in all the three projects have reduced considerably with time. This can be taken as the sure sign of maturity of the project. In the initial stages of the projects, the users request many features and the testers discover many bugs. Therefore, in any project, the activity will behigh at the start. As the time progresses, the product becomes stable and the number of tasks reduces. This can be clearly seen in the results.

Time Taken for Task Completion

The time taken to complete the tasks is also captured in the Table 1. The number of days taken to complete a task is a sure sign of the activity occuring in a project. It is expected that in Top Ranked projects, the time for completing tasks beless. The procedure for finding the time taken for task completion for a project P is as follows:

```
FOR i in (1 to 54)
DO
FOR ALL in Project_Task
DO
IF(Project_Task[i].Project_Group_ID=P)
DO
                P_Days[i] = (End_Date - Start_Date)/ 86400
      DONE
      DONE
DONE
```

This procedure was applied only for three Top Ranked projects with the ids 184122 and 176962. The results are given in Figure 2. Therefore, it is clear that one of the sure sign of a successful FOSS project is the reduced number of tasks over a period of time and reduction in the number of days required to complete the tasks in the project.

Task Allocation to Developers

The previous sections covered the issues of number of tasks and time taken to complete the tasks in Top Ranked projects. The number of tasks and the time taken to complete them were found to decrease with time thereby demonstrating the maturity of the project. In this section, the issue of task allocation in the Top Ranked projects isanalysed.

One of the attractions of development process in FOSS projects is the ability of developers to select the task they are interested to contribute. Unlike in the traditional development methodologies where task allocation is done in top down manner, FOSS projects envision developers picking the tasks voluntarily.

The analysis of projects shows that there is a method followed in allocation of tasks to developers. The core development team distributes the task of development among the members of the group. This strict allocation principle becomes necessary for a variety of reasons. Firstly, a developer may be the maintainer of the module for which changes are required. Secondly, the identified person may be the only person who has access permission to make the required changes to the source code of themodule. The data regarding the task assignment is captured in Table 1 and Table 2. The process of finding the pattern of task allocation for a project P in a given month i is given below.

```
FOR ALL in Project_Task
DO
```

Figure 1. Number of tasks

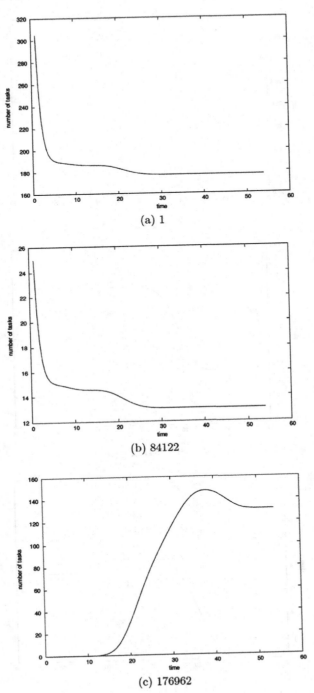

(a) 1

(b) 84122

(c) 176962

Figure 2. Time taken to complete the tasks

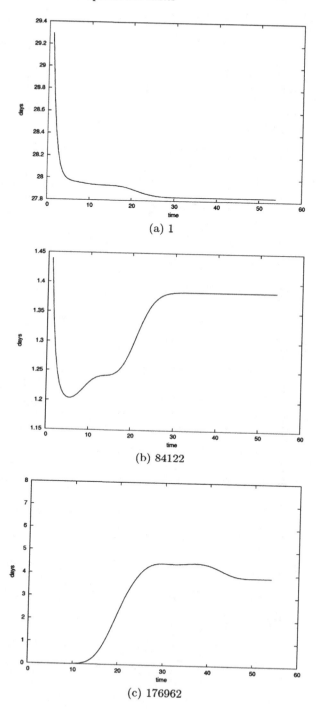

(a) 1

(b) 84122

(c) 176962

```
IF(Project_Task[i].Project_Group_ID= P)
DO
x[i]=Project_Task[i].created_by
DONE DONE
FOR ALL in Project_Assigned_To
y[i]=Project_Assigned_To[i]. assigned_to_id
```

The co-ordinates (x,y) thus obtained are used to plot a graph with each vertex representing the developer and an edge denoting a task allottedby a developer to the other. The undirected graphs thus represent the relationship between developers. The results obtained for the month of August 2009 are shown in Figure 3, Figure 4 and Figure 5.

The results clearly show a skewed pattern of developer involvement in these projects. In Chapter 4, Table 4 lists the total number of developers in the Top Ranked projects. According to the data available in that list, project id 1 has 68 developers. But Figure 3 captures the interaction between only 17 developers. Therefore, only 25% of the total developers in this project are allocated some task.

Similarly, project id 84122 has 37 and project id 176962 has 143 developers according to previous results. But the present analysis shows task allocation to only 7 and 36 developers respectively. Therefore, the amounts of developers who are allocated some task in these projects are 19% and 25% respectively.

Task Completion by Developers

The previous section showed that a very small number of developers are allotted tasks in the projects. But the successful implementation of the allotted task was not studied. In this section, the extent to which a developer completes the task assigned to him is studied. This becomes one of the crucial factors in FOSS projects because of the volunteer nature of developer contribution.

In the traditional software development environment, the issue of tracking the progress of the allocated tasks is done using various techniques such as Gantt chart. In a real time, deadline oriented development environment, a small variation from the predefined timeline will affect the progress of the complete system. But in a uncontrolled environment of FOSS development, the developers are not bound to complete the tasks that are allotted to them by their peers. But given the sustained success rate of the FOSS projects, it is assumed that the developers will successfully complete the responsibility given to them by the development team. The data regarding the task assignment is captured in Table 1and Table 2.

Table 2. Structure of table PROJECT ASSIGNED TO

Column	Type	Modifiers
Project_assigned_id	integer	not null defaultnextval
Project_task_id	integer	not null default 0
Assigned_to_id	integer	not null default 0

Figure 3. Task Allocation in Project-1

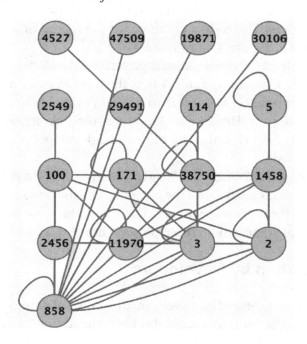

  The procedure for calculating the extent of task completion for a project P in a given month i is given below.

```
FOR ALL in Project_Task
DO
IF(Project_Task[i].Project_Group_ID= P)
DO
x[i] = Project_Task[i].project_task_id
IF(Project_Task[i].percent_complete= 100)
DO
y[i] = Project_Task[i].project_task_id
FOR ALL in Project_Assigned_To
d[i] = Project_Assigned_To[i].assigned_to_id
```

Table 3. Task Allocation in Projects (Aug 09)

Project Id	Total Developers	Developers Who Are Allotted Tasks
1	68	17
84122	37	7
176962	143	36

Figure 4. Task allocation in project-84122

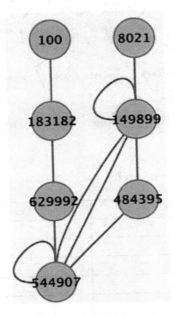

```
DONE
DONE
Percent_Complete[d] = [COUNT(y) / COUNT(x)] * 100
DONE
```

The results obtained by applying the above procedure to the data of August 2009 are given in Table 4, Table 5 and Table 6.

The result for project id 1 shows how effectively the volunteers contribute to FOSS development. The previous section had identified that out of 68 developers in this project, only 17 developers are allotted any task. The present analysis reveals that only three developers complete more than 10% of the work allotted work successfully. Therefore only 4% of total developers

Figure 5. Task allocation in project-176962

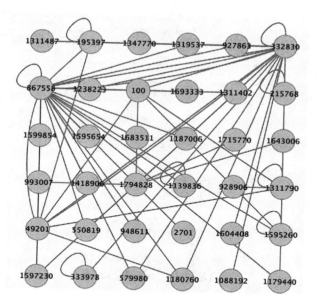

Table 4. Task completed in project-1

Developer	Task Completed (Percent)
114	0
19871	0
30106	0
2549	2
29491	3
171	4
2456	4
3	6
2	8
100	9
38750	10
11970	18
858	29

Table 5. Task completed in project-84122

Developer	Task Completed (Percent)
8021	1
149899	3
100	17
544907	77

Table 6. Task completed in project-176962

Developer	Task Completed (Percent)
1604408	0
1179440	1
1595260	1
1643006	1
867558	1
948611	1
993007	1
1715770	2
1139836	3
1311487	3
1319537	3
1597230	3
100	7
579980	9
1180760	11
195397	15
332830	29

actually complete more than 10% of allotted work thereby contributing to the development of the project which they subscribe to.

The analysis of project id 84122 and project id 176962 also shows similar trends. In project id 84122 only 2 developers complete more than 10% of allotted work successfully. Since the total numbers of developers in this project are 37, only 5% of developers can be called as contributing developers. In project id 176962, since the total number of developers is 143 and number of developers who complete more than 10% of allotted work successfully is 3, the amount of contributing developers is 2%.

Table 7. Task completion in projects (Aug 09)

Project Id	Total Developers	Developers Who Are Allotted tasks	Developers Who Complete More Than 10% of Allotted tasks
1	68	17	3
84122	37	7	2
176962	143	36	3

If the number of developers to whom tasks are allotted and the number of developers who complete their task successfully is taken together, we find that in project id 1, 17% of developers who are allotted task finish it successfully. In project id 84122 the corresponding figure is 28% and in project id 176962 it is 8%.

The results are summarised in Table 7.

CONCLUSION

The analysis of Three Top Ranked Projects from Feb 2005 to Aug 2009 yields following results

1.   The number of tasks in projects decreases with time
2.   The amount of time taken to complete the task decreases with time
3.   23% of developers are allotted tasks in a project
4.   20% of developers complete more than 10% of allotted tasks successfully
5.   4% of total developers actively contribute to project by completing the tasks allotted to them

Chapter 5
Exploratory Analysis of Free and Open Source Software Ecology

ABSTRACT

Shared repositories provide a host of services to start and sustain a FOSS project. They also share the details of projects with researchers. Sourceforge. net is a popular and populous forge with total number of projects exceeding 400,000 and developers counting more than 3 million as of Jan 2015. The evolution of this forge is studied and it was found that there is a small slide in the number of developers since September 2011. The existence of power law in Sourceforge.net is confirmed. The visualisation of developer relations reveal that there is a separate core and periphery groups of developers in Sourceforge.net and this trend was found to repeat in other forges like Freecode and Rubyforge.

INTRODUCTION

Free and Open Source Software (FOSS) is characterised mainly by its licensing terms. The Free Software licences and Open Source licences, though different in their relationship with commercial software, together provides an alternate model of software distribution. But FOSS is also important for the development model it follows. The success of FOSS lies in demonstrating the feasibility of developing a complex artefact like software by involving

DOI: 10.4018/978-1-5225-3707-6.ch005

global set of volunteers and using Internet as a communication medium. Ranging from a lone developer to literally tens of thousands of people and organisation, FOSS ecology today is probably world's largest virtual software development entity. But it is not necessary that any person or organisations who want to develop FOSS must follow this process. They can develop the software in-house without involving public but still release the software under FOSS licences.

Given the advantages of public participation model as demonstrated by success of GNU-Linux, many FOSS projects are developed in similar way. In the early days of GNU project and even during the initial stages of GNU-Linux development, the project leader would normally release the source code to public. Interested people would download, use, test, find bugs and then either reported or send fixes to the leader. The leader would have final say regarding the inclusion of bug fixes and new features. This model of development is still followed today but in place of a single leader there is a team which is normally formalised in all mature FOSS projects.

One of the major contributions of FOSS which is normally understudied is how much it has contributed towards the system and software development tools. Given the fact that most developers are mainly involved in FOSS to write software for their own use, this is quite natural. The growth of Internet coupled with the spread of computers during late 1990's enabled much larger participation in FOSS projects. This necessitated a mechanism which can automate the build and release processes. Separately there was a need for a communication platform beyond usenet and irc which could connect developers and end users. Bug reporting, feature request and general support also needed to be supported. Therefore, FOSS projects slowly started moving away from niche environments to public platform like Internet.

Mature and popular projects mostly host their projects in dedicated websites which support a range of features for efficient project management. Almost all technical and pubic communication details of the projects hosted in these sites are available for researchers. But given the fact that many FOSS projects start with single developer, it is not practical for every project to have its own website with all features. Also, the visibility of a project decreases if it works independently. Therefore, there exists multiple repositories which provide common facilities required to start and sustain a software project. They also provide a platform for developers to interact with projects they are interested. This multiplicity effect attracts many developers and organisations to host their projects in such repositories which are also called as forges.

In accordance with the promise of public development model of FOSS, such forges make the data regarding the projects hosted by them available for researchers. Mining Software Repositories has become a standard research topic providing a host of interesting issues to work upon. The software engineering researchers have access to such exhaustive data sets for first time and there are many opportunities to learn about software development process. Design, quality assurance and project management studies today include data from FOSS forges. The richness of data which include communication details is attracting researchers from rainbow domains like anthropology, sociology, economics, law and political science. Together they are trying to interpret this wonder phenomenon where gifted programmers seem to work without pay to create industry grade software and then distribute it at no cost along with source code without any restrictions on further use, modification and redistribution.

Evolution of Sourceforge.net

Sourceforge.net is probably more well known and one of the biggest FOSS repositories. As on Jan 2015 it hosts 400,000 projects and has 3 million registered users. Several high-profile projects like Vlc player, eMule are hosted in this site. It shares the data regarding projects hosted in the site with researchers through University of Norte Dam, USA.

SourceForge.net uses relational databases to store project management activity and statistics. There are over 100 relations (tables) in the data dumps provided to Notre Dame. Some of the data have been removed for security and privacy reasons. The Notre Dame researchers have built a data warehouse comprised of these monthly dumps, with each stored in a separate schema. Thus, each monthly dump is a snapshot of the status of all the SourceForge.net projects at that point in time.

The data dump of each month is identified as sfmmyy. Therefore, the dump of Jan 2013 is referred as sf0113. The tables in each dump are referred by the dump identifier and table name. So, the table 'artifact' for the month Oct 2013 should be referred as 'sf0913.artifact'. To facilitate the access of data, University of Notre Dame has provided a web access for the researchers to run sql queries on the data and download the result files in many formats.

For the purpose of present study, the data from Feb 2005 to Feb 2013 (sf0205-sf0213) is considered. Therefore, total of 96 datasets each containing around 100 tables is analysed. In some cases, the datasets for July 2007 (sf0707) and August 2007 (sf0807) were not considered because the data for these months were not in line with the historical trend. Repeated attempts to extract data from the data warehouse of University of Notre Dame gave the same erroneous results.

Therefore, it was concluded that these data are corrupted and should not be considered for present work.

The growth of projects and developers in Sourceforge.net is shown in Figure 1. The evolution of Sourceforge.net can be traced in three stages. The first period was 2005-2008 when the developers and projects were growing at a steady rate. 2009-2011 was the second period when there was a rapid growth of developers and projects. During September 2011, there was a dramatic shift in Sourceforge.net. For first time, the numbers of projects outnumbered the developers. It is beyond the scope of the present work to analyze the reasons behind this shift but we note that this is an important event which deserves much closer examination. One of the reasons for this trend may be the emergence of newer forges like github which began to attract more attention since 2010 onwards. But what is perplexing is the growth of projects. If developers are deserting Sourceforge.net why are the projects increasing at a healthy rate? Will be an interesting question to investigate further.

Figure 1. Developer and project growth in Sourceforge.net

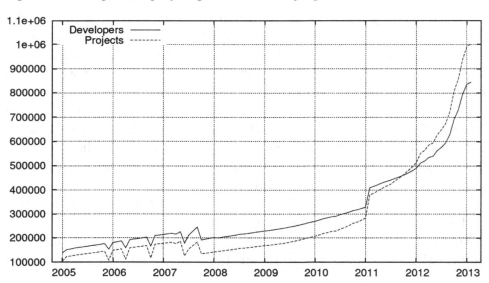

Visualisations of Developer Relations in Source-Forge.net

The Principle Component Analysis of Sourceforge.net as shown in Figure 2 confirms that number of developers in a project is an important measure of its success. Figure 3 shows that there exists power law in Sourceforge. net meaning there is a large set of developers working on small number of projects. Or in other words there is large number of projects which have small number of developers. To study this matter further there is a need to understand developer relations in Sourceforge.net.

Sourceforge.net maintains the developer and project details in the relation USER GROUP. The attribute USER ID is the unique code assigned to each registered user who is labelled as developer in present work and GROUP ID is the unique code of project to which the developer has subscribed. In order

Figure 2. Principle component analysis of Sourceforge.net

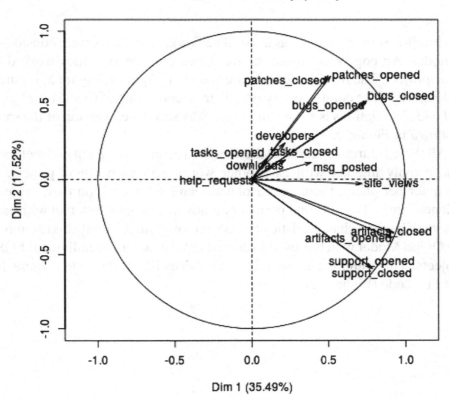

Figure 3. Power law in Sourceforge.net

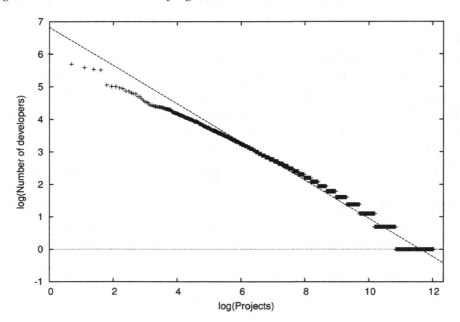

to visualise Sourceforge.net as a social network, developers were considered as nodes. An edge was present between two developers if they worked on same project. The resulting graphs are shown in Figure 4, Figure 5, Figure 6 and Figure 7. The complete network diagram consisting of 67565 developers and 643204 relations is shown in Figure 8. A simplified version of the same is shown in Figure 9.

All these figures suggest that there exists a central core team of developers who heavily interact with each other working in each others project. In the outer periphery, there exist isolated teams who work on their projects independently. The core and periphery teams who seldom interact with each other are the main characteristic of FOSS ecology. Surprisingly this resembles the Onion Model which is used to describe the structure of individual FOSS projects. This trend is also seen in other forges like Rubyforge (Figure 10) and Freecode (Figure 11).

Figure 4. Developer relations in Sourceforge.net for n=10000

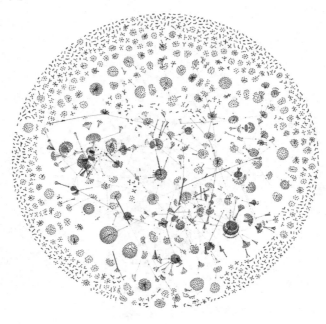

Figure 5. Developer relations in Sourceforge.net for n=20000

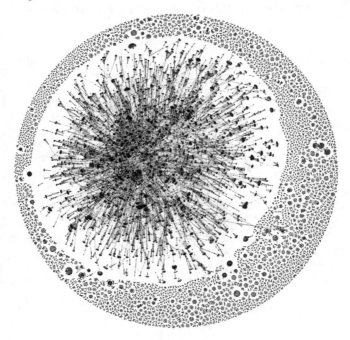

Figure 6. Developer relations in Sourceforge.net for n=30000

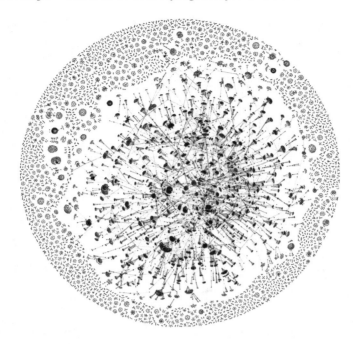

Figure 7. Developer relations in Sourceforge.net for n=40000

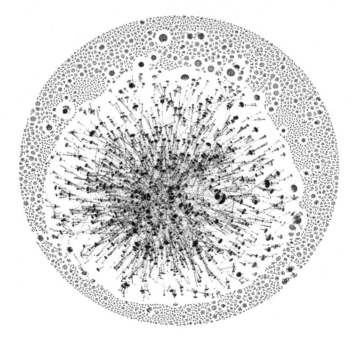

Figure 8. Developer relations in Sourceforge.net for n=67565

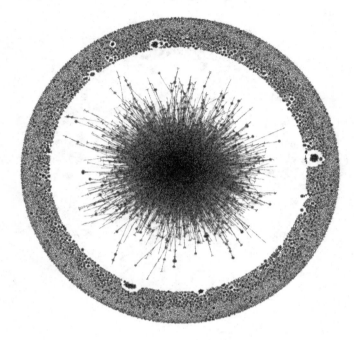

Figure 9. Refined developer relations in Sourceforge.net for n=67565

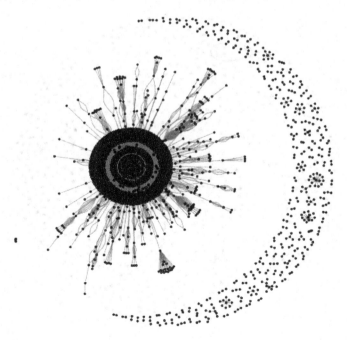

Figure 10. Developer relations in rubyforge

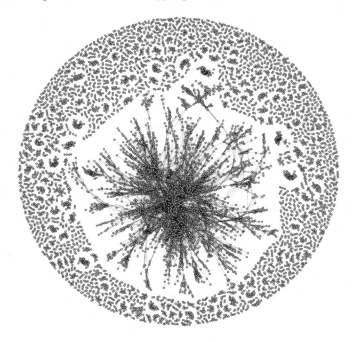

Figure 11. Developer relations in freecode

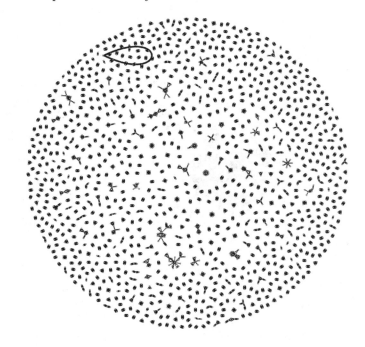

CONCLUSION

All these visualizations conclude that there exists a core team of developers who interact with each other working in each others project and the outer periphery there exist isolated teams who work on their projects independently. The core and periphery teams who seldom interact with each other are the main characteristic of FOSS ecology. Surprisingly this resembles the Onion Model which is used to describe the structure of individual FOSS projects.

Chapter 6

Finding Influential Nodes in Sourceforge.net Using Social Network Analysis

ABSTRACT

The contribution of volunteers in the development of Free and Open Source Software in Sourceforge.net is studied in this paper. Using Social Network analysis, the small set of developers who can maximize the information flow in the network are discovered. The propagation of top developers across past three years are also studied. The four algorithms used to find top influential developers gives almost similar results. The movement of top developers over past years years was also consistent.

INTRODUCTION

Social Network Analysis (SNA) has been an important tool for analyzing vari- ous domains of human behaviour. By bringing human interactions into graph structures they have helped gain new insights. Basic measures like betweenness, centrality, cohesion, reach etc can unveil lot of information about the modelled scenario. Concepts like 'Small World Phenomenon' are empirically verified across different cases. With the emergence of new computational tools there has been renewed interest in the application of Social Network Analysis into new domains. FOSS is primarily a global network of volunteers and thus makes for an ideal case to study using SNA

DOI: 10.4018/978-1-5225-3707-6.ch006

Tools. The rich research available in SNA can be helpful in understanding the complex phenomenon which makes FOSS work. The present work focuses on one aspect of SNA namely the influence maximization problem. The main objective here is to find a small set of most influential nodes in a social network so that their aggregated influence in the network is maximized. In the context of FOSS, the most influential nodes correspond to developers who are very well connected in FOSS ecology and therefore have maximum chance to propagate information in the network. Four well known algorithms namely High Degree, LDAG, SPS-CELF++ and SimPath are used to find top 5 influential developers. The propagation of top developers during past three years are also studied.

Early attempts of applying social network analysis to Free and Open Source Software phenomenon was undertaken by studying the properties such as degree distribution, diameter, cluster size and clustering coefficient. The emergence of the small world phenomenon in such networks was also studied (Xu, Christley, & Madey, 2006). The issue of finding the most influential nodes in social networks is treated in the literature as problem of centrality. In one of earliest comprehensive study on the centrality of social networks nine centrality measures were proposed. Among them three were based on degrees of points, next three on betweenness of points and last three on closeness. These different conceptions give three different views of centrality namely control, independence and activity (Freeman, 1979). The first natural greedy strategy solution which performed better than node selection heuristics based on notions of degree centrality and distance centrality continues to influence the studies in this domain (Kempe, Kleinberg & Tardos, 2003). A greedy algorithm for the target set selection problem where an initial set of nodes are selected to maximize the propagation in a social network was also proposed by same authors (Kempe, Kleinberg, & Tardos, 2005).

The later works have used variety of approaches to find top-k nodes in social networks. Finding top influential nodes using bond percolation method is tried (Kimura, Saito & Nakano, 2007). Using the metaphor of 'Outbreak Detection' the problem of informa- tion diffusion was discussed in different way. The novel solution was proposed as CELF algorithm which is reported to perform 700 times faster than simple greedy algorithm (Leskovec et al., 2007). Effective heuristics derived from the independent cascade model was comparable or better then greedy algorithms in finding top nodes for influ- ence maximization problem (Chen, Wang & Yang, 2009). Most of the studies on influence maximization assume single degree of influence across the network. In contrast, the study of topic level social influence on large networks is also undertaken (Tang et al., 2009). A novel algorithm using the concept of Shapley value from cooperative game theory is also proposed to find top influential nodes in social network (Narayanam & Narahari, 2010).

Greedy algorithm for mining top-K influential nodes which works by identifying communities within the network and then detecting the influential nodes is also reported (Wang et al., 2010). A recent attempt to improve the CELF algorithm by exploiting the property of submodularity of the spread function for influence propagation models is reported as SPS-CELF++ (Goyal, Lu, & Lakshmanan, 2011). While most solutions for influence maximization depend on the social graph structure a data based approach using historical data and avoiding the need for learning influence probabilities is also proposed by same authors (Goyal, Bonchi & Lakshmanan, 2011). They also propose another efficient algorithm SIMPATH for influence maximization under the linear threshold model (Goyal, Lu & Lakshmanan, n.d.). The first scalable influence maximization algorithm specific for the linear threshold model was proposed using LDAG algorithm (Chen, Yuan & Zhang, 2010). Identifying influential nodes using Principal Component Centrality is also proposed (Ilyas & Radha, 2011). A comprehensive survey of the development in this area is also reported (Bonchi, 2011).

Finding Top-k Developers

The crucial aspect in social network analysis is to determine the weight of the edges in the graph. For the present discussion, the weight of an edge corresponds to the influence a node has on related node. Instead of randomly assigning the edge weight two methods were contemplated. The first was to use outdegree of each node as a means to determine influence of each node as follows:

$$Influence_{A \rightarrow B} = 1 \Big/ deg^+(A)$$

where in graph

$deg^+(v) \leftarrow out\_degree \ of \ developer\_no\_dev$

The above method has a shortcoming that all related nodes will be assigned same weight. That means if a developer is working on many projects it is assumed that he is equally active in all projects. In a more realistic scenario as a developer involves himself in more number of projects his contribution to each of those should decline. Therefore, a different method to calculate the weight of the influence called 'Shared Project Model' was formulated. The Procedure to calculate influence edge from developer node A to node B is as follows:

$$Influence_{A \to B} = w * \frac{|P_A|}{|U_{ab}|}$$

where $w = \sum_{p \in I_{ab}} \frac{1}{|p|}$

$U_{ab} = P_A \cup P_B$

$I_{ab} = P_A \cap P_B$

$P_X \leftarrow \{p_1, p_2, p_3 \cdots p_n\}$ where p_i is a project of developer X

The partial structure of the graph thus obtained is shown in Table 2. This was used to find the top-5 influential nodes using the four algorithms High Degree, LDAG, SPS-CELF++ and SimPath. The result obtained for the month of Dec 2011 is given in Table 3. As it can be seen from the results except High Degree all algorithms almost give same results for top two nodes. The developer with id 2909886 emerges as the top most influential developer. This set of developers can be considered as seed nodes for maximizing the information flow in the sourgeforge.net community. This has huge implications regarding targeted marketing campaigns or simple information dissemination among the developer community.

The runtime performances of these four algorithms are given in Figure 1 and Figure 2. LDAG algorithm trades memory for speed because it constructs LDAG for each node. HighDegree requires very little computation over represen- tation of the graph in memory. The parameters used for each algorithm are k = 20 and the propagation model is Linear Threshold. LDAG has threshold of 1/320, Cutoff for SimPath and SPS-CELF++ is 0.001 and its topl is 4 for Look Ahead Optimization.

$$G = (V, E, b) \hspace{6cm} [1]$$

$$S \leftarrow \varnothing$$

Find the k nodes with the highest out-degree(deg^+) and add each node to set S

```
S
[1]
/* preparation phase */
S = ∅
∀v ∈ V, IncInf (v) = 0
each node v ∈ V
generate LDAG(v, θ)
/* Inf Set(v)'s are derived from LDAG(v, θ)'s */
∀u ∈LDAG(v, θ), set ap_v (u) = 0
∀u ∈LDAG(v, θ), compute α_v (u)
each u in LDAG(v, θ)
IncInf (u)+ = α_v (u)
/* main loop for selecting k seeds */ i = 1 to k
```
$$s = \arg\max_{v \in V \setminus S} \{IncInf\ (v)\}$$
```
each v ∈ Inf Set(s)\S
/* update α_v (u) for all u's that can reach s in LDAG(v, θ) */
Δα_v (s) = -α_v (s); ∀u ∈ S, Δα_v (u) = 0
```

Topologically sort all nodes that can reach s in LDAG(v, θ) in a sequence ρ, with s sorted first. Compute $\Delta\alpha_v (u)$ for all $u \in \rho$), where $\rho \setminus (S \cup \{v\})$ is replaced by $\rho \setminus (S \cup \{s\})$ and $\alpha_v ()$ is replaced by $\Delta\alpha_v ()$.

```
α_v (u)+ = Δα_v (u), for all u ∈ ρ
IncInf (u)+ = Δα_v (u) · (1 - ap_v (u)) for all u ∈ ρ
/* Update ap_v (u) for all u's reachable from s in LDAG(v, θ) */
Δap_v (s) = 1 - ap_v (s); ∀u ∈ S, Δap_v (u) = 0
```

Topologically sort all nodes reachable from s in LDAG(v, θ) into a sequence ρ, with s sorted first. compute $\Delta ap_v (x)$ for all $u \in \rho$, where $\rho \setminus S$ is replaced by $\rho \setminus (S \cup \{s\})$ and $ap()$ is replaced by $\Delta ap_v ()$

```
ap_v (u) += Δap_v (u), for all u ∈ ρ
IncInf (u) - = α_v (u) · Δap_v (u) for all u ∈ ρ
S = S ∪ {s}
S
[1] G, k seed set S
```

```
S ← ∅; Q ← ∅; last seed = null; cur best = null.
each u ∈ V
u.mg1 = σ({u}; u.prev best = cur best; u.mg2 = σ({u, cur
best}); u.flag = 0.
Add u to Q. update cur best based on mg1.
|S| < k
u = top (root) element in Q. u.flag == |S|
S ← S ∪ {u}; Q ← Q - {u}; last seed = u.
continue; u.prev best == last seed
u.mg1 = u.mg2.
u.mg1 = Δ_u(S); u.prev best = cur best; u.mg2 = Δ_u(S ∪ {cur
best}).
u.flag = |S|; Update cur_best
Reinsert u into Q and heapify.
[1] G = (V, E, b), η, l
```

Find the vertex cover of the input graph *G*. Call it *C*. each $u \in C$

```
U ← (V - C) ∩ N^{in}(u).
Compute α(u) and α^{v -v}, ∀v ∈ SIMPATH -SPREAD(u, η, U).
Add u to CELF queue.
each v ∈ V - C
Compute α(v) .
Add u to CELF queue.
S ← ∅. spd ← 0
|S| < k
U ← top-l node in CELF queue.
Compute α^{v -x}(S), ∀x ∈ SIMPATH-SPREAD(S, η, U).
each x ∈ U
x is previously examined in the current iteration
S ← S + x; Update spd.
Remove x from CELF queue. Break out of the loop.
Call BACKTRACK(x, η, V - S, ∅) to compute α^{v -s}(x).
Compute α(S + x) using Eq. 6
Compute marginal gain of u as α(S + x) - spd.
Re-insert u in CELF queue such that its other is maintained.
return S
```

The procedure mentioned above to find top 5 developers was applied to all datasets from Feb 2009 to Dec 2011. The results are shown in Figure 3, Figure 4, Figure 5 and Figure 6. The graphs show remarkable consistency of some developers to remain in top 5 positions over many years. This is an indication that the select group of developers remain active for long time thus confirming that few developers do most of the work in FOSS ecology (Raj & Srinivasa, 2011, 2012).

Table 1. Structure of Table USER_GROUP

Column	Type	Modifiers
User_group_id	integer	not null
User_id	integer	not null default 0
Group_id	integer	not null default 0
Admin_flags	character (16)	not null
Forum_flags	integer	not null default 0
Project_flags	integer	not null default 2
Doc_flags	integer	not null default 0
Member_role	integer	not null default 100
Release_flags	integer	not null default 0
Artifact_flags	integer	not null default 0
Added_by	integer	not null default 100
Grantcvs	integer	not null default 1
grantshell	integer	not null default 1
Row_modtime	integer	not null
News_flags	integer	not null default 0
Screenshot_flags	integer	not null default 0
Grantsvn	integer	not null default 1

Table 2. Structure of social network graph

Node1	Node2	Edge Weight
0	51680	0.222222
0	16458	0.222222
1	60747	0.500000
2	19263	0.133333
2	21267	0.057143
2	30770	0.100000
2	20935	0.080000
3	22251	0.074074
3	6431	0.055556

Table 3. Top 5 developers in Dec 2011

Algorithm	Top Developers
High Degree	783089 405789 1632 11084 438768
LDAG	2909886 454395 11058 597819 918951
SPS-CELF++	2909886 454395 72656 45353 597819
SimPath	2909886 454395 72656 45353 597819

Figure 1. CPU utilization of algorithms

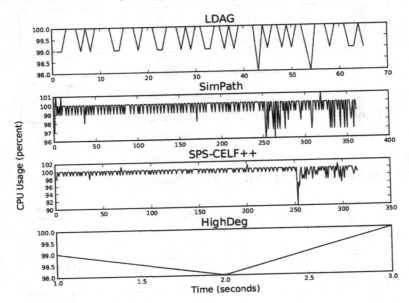

CONCLUSION

In this work, a novel attempt to find most influential nodes in the Free and Open Source Software developer network using Social Network Analysis approach was attempted. The influential developers were discovered using four different algo- rithms namely High Degree, LDAG, SPS-CELF++ and SimPath. It was found that except High Degree all other algorithms mostly agree on top developers. Identification of this influential set of developers is important because they can be the seed nodes for targeted marketing. The study of their movement across time line establishes the consistency of the top developers. Overall this work adds to the growing literature in this domain by making new contributions using theories from Social Network Analysis.

Figure 2. Memory utilization of algorithms

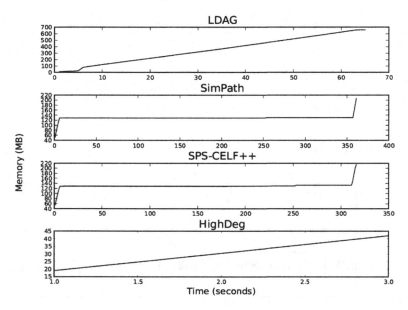

Figure 3. Top 5 developers: high degree algorithm

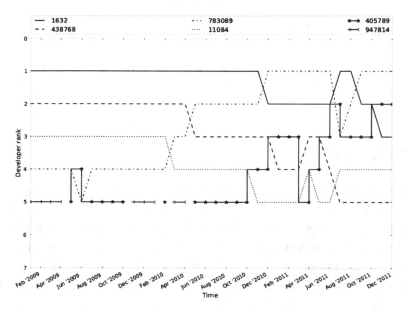

Figure 4. Top 5 developers: LDAG algorithm

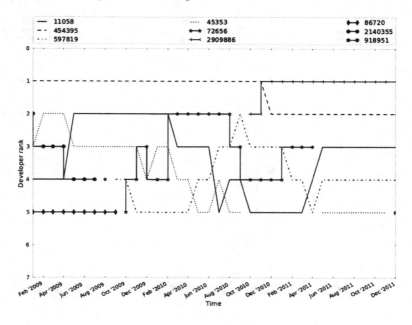

Figure 5. Top 5 developers: SPS-CELF++ algorithm

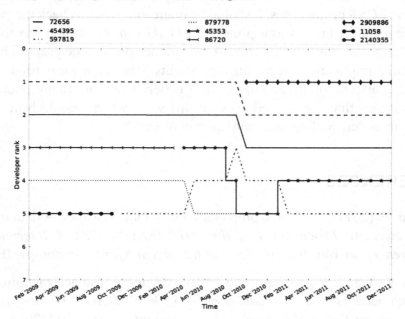

Figure 6. Top 5 developers: SimPath algorithm

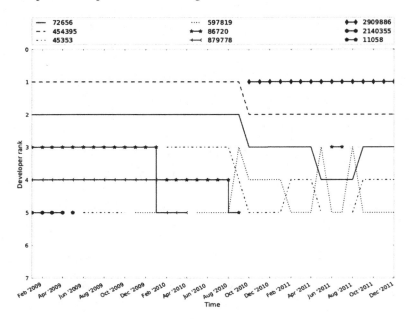

The future directions are to verify the presence of same results across different FOSS project sites. It should be interesting also to check the validity of these results in large, single project like GNU-Linux. Another way forward is to change the way weights are assigned to the edges in the graph. This can have huge implications regarding the results. The algorithms tried in this work can also be optimized to perform better. There are many interesting opportunities that are opened up with this work which should bring more clarity in understanding the phenomenon of FOSS.

REFERENCES

Bonchi, F. (2011). Influence propagation in social networks: A data mining perspective. In *Proceedings of the 2011 IEEE/WIC/ACM International Conferences on Web Intelligence and Intelligent Agent Technology*. IEEE.

Chen, W., Wang, Y., & Yang, S. (2009). Efficient influence maximization in social networks. In *Proceedings of the 15th ACM SIGKDD international conference on Knowledge discovery and data mining* (pp. 199–208). ACM.

Chen, W., Yuan, Y., & Zhang, L. (2010). Scalable influence maximization in social networks under the linear threshold model. In *Proceedings of the 2010 IEEE 10th International Conference on Data Mining (ICDM)* (pp. 88–97). IEEE.

Freeman, L. C. (1979). Centrality in social networks conceptual clarification. *Social Networks*, *1*(3), 215–239. doi:10.1016/0378-8733(78)90021-7

Goyal, A., Bonchi, F., & Lakshmanan, L. V. S. (2011). A data-based approach to social influence maximization. *Proceedings of the VLDB Endowment*, *5*(1), 73–84. doi:10.14778/2047485.2047492

Goyal, A., Lu, W., & Lakshmanan, L. V. S. (2011). Celf++: optimizing the greedy algorithm for influence maximization in social networks. In *Proceedings of the 20th international conference companion on World Wide Web* (pp. 47–48). ACM. doi:10.1145/1963192.1963217

Goyal, A., Lu, W., & Lakshmanan, L.V.S. (n.d.). Simpath: An efficient algorithm for influence maximization under the linear threshold model. Academic Press.

Ilyas, M. U., & Radha, H. (2011). Identifying influential nodes in online social networks using principal component centrality. In *Proceedings of the 2011 IEEE International Conference on Communications (ICC)*. IEEE.

Kempe, D., Kleinberg, J., & Tardos, E. (2003). Maximizing the spread of influence through a social network. In *Proceedings of the ninth ACM SIGKDD international conference on Knowledge discovery and data mining* (pp. 137-146). ACM. doi:10.1145/956750.956769

Kempe, D., Kleinberg, J., & Tardos, E. (2005). *Influential nodes in a diffusion model for social networks* (pp. 99–99). Automata, Languages and Programming. doi:10.1007/11523468_91

Kimura, M., Saito, K., & Nakano, R. (2007). Extracting influential nodes for information diffusion on a social network. In *Proceedings of the National Conference on Arificial Intelligence* (Vol. 22, p. 1371). London: AAAI Press.

Leskovec, J., Krause, A., Guestrin, C., Faloutsos, C., & VanBriesen, J. Glance (2007) - Cost-effective outbreak detection in networks. In *Proceedings of the 13th ACM SIGKDD international conference on Knowledge discovery and data mining* (pp. 420–429). ACM.

Narayanam, R., & Narahari, Y. (2010). A Shapley value-based approach to discover influential nodes in social networks. *IEEE Transactions on Automation Science and Engineering*, (99), 1–18.

Raj, P. M. K., & Srinivasa, K. G. (2011, March). Analysis of projects and volunteer participation in large scale free and open source software ecosystem. *ACM SIGSOFT Softw. Eng. Notes*, *36*.

Raj, P. M. K., & Srinivasa, K. G. (2012, March). Empirical studies of global volunteer collaboration in the development of free and open source software: Analysis of six top ranked projects in sourceforge.net. *ACM SIGSOFT Softw. Eng. Notes*, *36*, 1–5.

Tang, J., Sun, J., Wang, C., & Yang, Z. (2009). Social influence analysis in large-scale networks. In *Proceedings of the 15th ACM SIGKDD international conference on Knowledge discovery and data mining* (pp. 807–816). ACM. doi:10.1145/1557019.1557108

Wang, Y., Cong, G., Song, G., & Xie, K. (2010). Community-based greedy algorithm for mining top-k influential nodes in mobile social networks. In *Proceedings of the 16th ACM SIGKDD international conference on Knowledge discovery and data mining* (pp. 1039–1048). ACM. doi:10.1145/1835804.1835935

Xu, J., Christley, S., & Madey, G. (2006). Application of social network analysis to the study of open source software. Elsevier Press.

Chapter 7
Graph Mining Approaches to Study Volunteer Relationships in Sourceforge.net

ABSTRACT

The contribution of volunteers in the development of Free and Open Source Software in Sourceforge.net is studied in this paper. Using Social Network analysis, the small set of developers who can maximize the information flow in the network are discovered. The propagation of top developers across past three years are also studied. The four algorithms used to find top influential developers gives almost similar results. The movement of top developers over past years was also consistent. Influential nodes in a network are very important to diffuse influence on the rest of the network. They are most often highly connected within the network. The existing algorithms are efficient to identify them. However, the challenge is in selecting a seed set that can spread the influence instantaneously with least effort. In this paper, a method is defined to spread influence on the entire network by selecting the least number of non-overlapping influential nodes faster than a well known existing algorithm. Further to this, the number of clusters in the network is also determined simultaneously from the seed set of the networks.

DOI: 10.4018/978-1-5225-3707-6.ch007

INTRODUCTION

Increase in the use of personal computers in late 1980s has encouraged much wider use of Social network analysis (SNA) methods because it has meant increased ability to manage large data sets and to visualize social network data in a wide variety of ways (Pan, 2007). Social network analysis is based on an assumption of the importance of relationships among interacting units. It is also used to study social relations among a set of actors as it concerns with the network structure formulation and solution (Borgatti, Mehra, Brass et al., 2009; Carrington, Scott & Wasserman, 2005). Such structures are usually captured in graphs. At organisations, collaboration in networks is critical to innovation. Paradoxically these networks are taken for granted, frequently invisible and rarely managed (Lim, Quercia & Finkelstein, 2010; Thomas, Valluri & Karlapalem, 2006).

Social network analysis is focused on uncovering the patterning of people's interaction. A rapid growth in work across organisation as well as geographic boundaries with outsourcing, off-shoring, virtual organisations and business process networks combined with trends such as the rise of blogs, online communities and social networking sites such as Friendster and Linkedin as well as the rapid growth of collaborative software have all contributed to the emergence of SNA from the academic closet. The network's perspective encompasses theories, models, and applications that are expressed in terms of relational concepts or processes. Along with growing interest and increased use of network analysis has come a consensus about the central principles underlying the network perspective. The semantic web is an emerging concept that launches the idea of having data on the web defined and linked in a way that it can be used by people and processed by machines. The semantic web and social network models support each other (Jamali & Abolhassani, 2006).

Graph Data Mining in Social Network Analysis

Graphs have become very important in modelling complicated structures. Many domains produce data that can be intuitively represented by graphs. The process of discovering interesting facts and information about these graphs is difficult and challenging to work with, because real world data is very huge for any sort of raw interpretation. Graph mining which is a data mining approach has to be collaborated with SNA to obtain the results of the data sets so as to provide us with an insight of the frequent sub graphs of interest.

Influence Maximization Using Pagerank Algorithm

In a social network, the graph of relationships and interactions within a group of individuals plays a fundamental role as a medium for the spread of information, ideas and influence among its members. Influence maximization is the problem of finding a small subset of nodes (seed nodes) in a social network that could maximize the spread of influence. More formally, the influence maximization problem is the following. Given a probabilistic model for influence, determine a set A of k individuals yielding the largest expected cascade. The influence maxi- mization problem can be formulated as an optimization problem, given a network structure and an influence cascade model, which are two key factors affecting the outcome of an influence propagation. Several stochastic influence cascade models, namely the independent cascade model, the weight cascade model, and the linear threshold model are studied. Different Algorithms were used to compute influence maximization in social network, and they are adopted to fit parallel implemen- tation on many-core GPU. Effective performance benefits have been achieved by considering the terms that affects the GPU Performance (Seo, Kyong & Eun-Jin, 2012).

Nodes in the social network represent the actors of that network. Each node contributes to the whole network in a different way. The influence of a node depends on both local and global parameters. Local parameters are the outdegree or the connectedness of that node in the network and global parameters include the role or priority given to that actor and the position of that actor in a network. These parameters are responsible to determine the influence of a particular node in the social network (Kimura, Yamakawa, Saito et al., 2008). Influential nodes are those which play major roles and any changes to parameters related to them have the greater impact on the whole network. A node is highly influential if it is present in denser region and connected to many other nodes compare to the similar node present at the edges of the whole network. Exponential increase in the usage of social networks in the present world lead to large networks being analysed for most influential regions or the nodes. Knowledge about these nodes helps to understand the whole network and the activities in a better way and to take appropriate actions.

Data Set

The dataset used in the present work contains Developers - Developers relation data from Sourceforge.net, where the developers are represented by the unique developer IDs. A relation exists between two developer IDs only if both are involved in same project. Each developer can be involved in more than one project. In the graph format developers are represented by nodes or vertices and the relations between them are represented by the presence of edge between them. Table 1 shows the first 15 lines of the data set. Figure 1 shows the graphical representation of the same.

Page Rank algorithm addresses the Link-based Object Ranking (LOR) problem (Jain, Sharma, Dixit et al., 2013). The objective here is to assign a numerical rank or priority to each node by exploiting the link structure of the network. It starts a random walk from a node by randomly following links from the node it is present at any point. For example, Page Rank applied on a web gives the rank of each web page in- dicating the probability of that web page being visited on a particular random walk. Algorithm 3 presents the Page Rank algorithm which was on our dataset to assign the rank to each developer present in the network and thus find most influential developers in the network which is shown in Table 2.

Figure 1. Graphical representation of data set

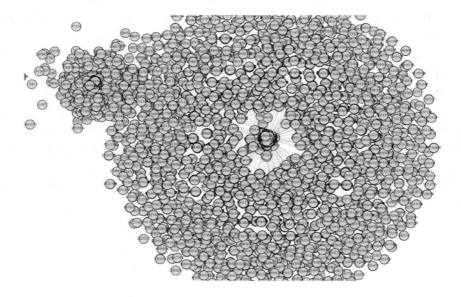

Table 1. Sample entries from the data set

2	5
159	5
2	100
2	858
3	100
3	114
3	171
3	858
5	100
858	2
2	2456
4500	2
7066	0
112	100
116	101

Table 2. PageRank for developer: developer data

Top 5 Influential Developer IDs in the Dataset
100, 918083, 1030194, 689404, 1768158

- **Input:** G-Directed graph of N Developers, d-Damping factor
- **Output:** $PR[1...N]$, where $PR[P_i]$ is the PageRank of page P_i

Let $PP[1...N]$ denote a spare array of size N

Let d denote the probability of reaching a particular node by a random jump either from a vertex with no outlinks or with probability $(1 - d)$

Let $N(P_u)^+$ denote set of pages with at least one outlink each P_i in N of G

$$PR[Pi] \leftarrow \frac{1}{n}\frac{1}{n}$$

$$PP[i] \leftarrow 0$$

PR not converging each P_i in N of G each P_i in N $(P_i)^+$ PP $[Pj] \leftarrow PP$ $[P_j]$ $+ (PR[Pi]) / \deg(P+i)$ $(PR[Pi]) / \deg(P+i)$ each P_i in N of G $PR[P_i] \leftarrow d / n$ $d / n + (1 - d)$ $(PP$ $[P_i])$

PP $[P_i] \leftarrow 0$

Normalize $PR[P_i]$ so that $\Sigma_{Pi \in N} PR[P_i] \leftarrow 1$

Link Prediction

Extrapolating knowledge or pattern of links in a given network to deduce novel links that are plausible, and may occur in the future is the purpose of Link Prediction (Cheng-Hao, Wan-Chuen, Cheng-Chi et al., 2013). Given a snapshot of a social network, it is possible to infer new interactions between members who have never interacted before. Link prediction applied to developer-developer relation dataset predicts the relations most probably occur in future based on developer interests in particular type of projects. Link prediction problems can be robustly handled by modelling it as classification problem. One of the major task is choosing feature set, therefore three efficient features introduced are:

- Proximity features;
- Aggregated features;
- Topological features (Thi & Hoang, 2013).

Simple set of easy to use structural features that can be analysed to identify missing links in social networks are explained. Friends' measure has been introduced and proved as an effective measure to find the missing links (Fire et al., 2011).

Problem Statement

An emperical study to predict the most probable relations among developers based on the already existing relations in the developer-developer relation network and to evaluate the performance measures of the link prediction algorithm.

Dataset

Input dataset is same as the one used for Page Rank explained in previous Section.

Procedure

Given a snapshot of a social network in a time interval t0 to t0, it is possible to accurately predict the edges that will be added to the network during the future interval from time t1 to t1 (Nowell & Kleinberg, 2003). The training set and the testing set are the graphs in the interval t0 to t0 and t1 to t1 which are given in Figure 2 and Figure 3, respectively. While predicting links based on distance metrics, we do not use external properties but make best use of features intrinsic to the graph to make judgments. From an SNA standpoint, chances of a person making a new friend in the future are high if the new person happens to be an existing friend's friend, thereby making him/her a mutual friend. This notion of closeness is what needs to be searched for in a graph.

Figure 2. Training graph data

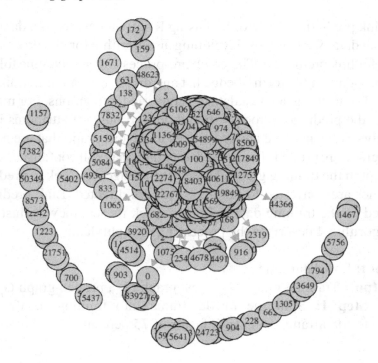

Figure 3. Test graph data

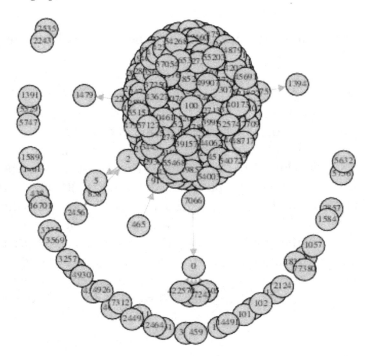

The link prediction is performed using R software which is a data mining tool for big data. We begin by developing an algorithm for pre-processing the raw data for link prediction. The graph pre-processing involves the following: Accept raw-data in the form of edge list and divide the data into training and test data. The training and test data are converted into graphs. For maximum accuracy, the prediction process should depend only on attributes intrinsic to the network. Hence, the newer vertices in the test graph that are not in the training graph are pruned. The pruned test graph may still contain newer edges not present in the training graph. These are the edges we seek to predict. The data frames are converted to graphs which are directed. Link prediction is performed on the training data to finally check its accuracy against the test data. Algorithm 4 describes the processing of input data.

- **Input:** Rawdataframe
- **Output:** Training graph G_{train}, test graph G_{test}, pruned graph G_{prune}
  - **Step 1:** Split the rawdataframe into training dataframe and testdataframe using split factor of 75 percent.

- ○ **Step 2:** Convert data frames into graphs.
- ○ **Step 3:** Prune test data so that nodes intrinsic to the network are only used.

To obtain the probable links we need to use proximity measures (Murata & Moriyasu, 2007) (Liben-Nowell & Kleinberg, 2007). A proximity measure gives the measure of influence of nodes with respect to the location in the data set. The proximity measures used are in current work are Similarity Measure and Dissimilarity Measure also known as the Distance Mea- sure. Similarity measure works using the principle of Shared Nearest Neighbours (SNN). According to SNN, pair of nodes are more similar compare to other pairs if they share more common neighbours in comparison to other pairs. The similarity values range between [0-1] and the value closer are to 1 indicate more similarity. The other proximity measure used is Dissimilarity or Distance Mea- sure which is also based on SNN. The dissimilarity values also range between [0-1] and the value closer to 1 indicates more dissimilarity. Threshold used is contradictory to the similarity measure.

The results obtained will be huge because of the enormous size of the data set. Applying a suitable threshold will prune away all the redundant pair-wise computations and the most probable links can be found. To avoid ambiguity with decimal values, Boolean values can be used to differentiate among the values that lie above and below the threshold respectively. A suitable threshold for Similarity Measure would be 0.75 and that for Distance Measure would be 0.25. This will considerably eliminate the redundant pairwise values. The training data is converted to a predicted graph. Both the proximity measures can be computed by using three different methods namely, Euclidean, Jaccard and Correlation.

- **[H] Input:** Training graph $G(V, E)$, threshold
- **Output:** Prediction adjacency matrix
  - ○ **Step 1:** Apply similarity or dissimilarity measure on training graph with the method.
  - ○ **Step 2:** Convert results above threshold to 1.
  - ○ **Step 3:** Resultspredicted Graph.

The predicted graph is the result of the computation of proximity measures on the training data. This has to be evaluated against the test data graph to check for correctness. The performance metrics used are:

- **TP** = Number of edges present in predicted graph AND present in test graph.
- **TN** = Number of edges not present in predicted graph AND present in test graph.
- **FP** = Number of edges present in predicted graph AND not present in test graph.
- **FN** = Number of edges not present in predicted graph AND not present in test graph.

By using these performance metrics, we can evaluate the performance of the link prediction algorithm by measuring the accuracy, recall and precision. Preci- sion is the probability that a (randomly selected) retrieved document is relevant. Recall is the probability that a (randomly selected) relevant document is retrieved in a search. Accuracy is the ratio of the true relations in the data set to the entire population of the data set. The results are shown in Table 3 and Table 4.

- **[H] Input:** Predicted graph $G(V, E)$
- **Output:** TP, FP, TN, FN, precision, recall, accuracy
  - **Step 1:** Compare predicted matrix with converted pruned matrix.
  - **Step 2:** Get tp = links present in both the graphs, tn = links present in pruned graph and not in predicted graph, fp = links present in predicted graph and not pruned graph, fn = links not present in both.
  - **Step 3:** Calculate $precision = tp \,/\, tp + fp$.

$$recall = tp/\left(tp + fn\right)$$

$$accuracy = tp + tn \,/\, tp + fp + tn + fn$$

Table 3. Dissimilarity measures

Measure	Precision	Recall	Accuracy
Euclidean	0.007673847	50.75655	39.56315
Jaccard	0.00687702	38.24719	49.1792

Frequent Subgraph Mining

Mining of frequent patters has been an active field in data mining. in graphs patterns are usually mined with the help of vertices and edges. Frequent subgraph mining can be used in many different aspects such as fraud detection and finding most flexible employee. In fraud detection, the pattern will help us predict the next move whereas in set of employees, most active employee can be determined. The heart of frequent subgraph mining is graph/subgraph isomorphism test (Nijssen & Kok, 2005; Kuramochi & Karypis, 2001). The Apriori-like algorithms which are commonly used suffer two major costs:

1.   Costly subgraph isomorphism test.
2.   Costly candidate generation. gSpanis an algorithm without candidate generation, therefore it takes care of both the issues (Yan & Han, 2002).

More formally, given a labelled graph G = (V, E, L, l) where V is a set of vertices, E is a set of edges, L is a set of labels and l is the function assigning labels to vertices and edges, the goal of Frequent Subgraph Mining is to find every graph g, such that sum of 0's and 1's (g is 1 if isomorphic else 0) is greater than or equal to minimum support.

- **Input:** A graph database D, and the minimum support, min support.
- **Output:** The set of frequent subgraph S.

S all frequent one edge subgraphs in D SortSinlexicographicorder n ∈ *N* Call gSpan- Expansion (D, n, min_support, S)

Remove *n from D* **return** S

n ≠ min gSpan_Encoding(n) Return Add *ntoS* e such that e is a single edge rightmost expansion of nsupport(e) ≥ *min support, S* Call gSpanExpansion(D, n, min_support, S)

Table 4. Similarity measures

Measure	Precision	Recall	Accuracy
Correlation	0.01337016	49.16854	66.39712
Jaccard	0.01136599	49.16854	60.47193

Initially an input with vertex labels and a minimum support threshold is given. First the algorithms remove infrequent vertices and edges from the graph set. Then it finds all single edge subgraphs and sort them in lexicographic order. If the support of any single edge subgraph is less than minimum support, it will be eliminated. The remaining frequent single edge subgraphs become the seeds to grow bigger subgraphs. Now second algorithm begins recursively extending the edge subgraphs found above using rightmost expansion. The final result shows the most frequently occurring graphs by displaying the vertices (labels) and edges (labels).

SUBDUE Algorithm

The application of FSM algorithms to real world problems has prompted re- searchers to apply heuristics that limit the search space to only interesting subgraphs. The most widely used of these heuristic algorithms is SUBDUE. It is fast and uses Beam search and compression methodologies. The concepts in SUBDUE are as follows:

1. **Beam Search:** Its best first version of breadth first search.
2. **Minimum Description Length:** Compression is representing data using a smaller number of bits. The DL of a graph G is denoted DL(G) The value of it is the integer number of bits required to represent graph G in binary format.

SUBDUE algorithm given in Algorithm starts with the set of all one vertex subgraphs, the original parents. Each parent is extended in all possible ways. SUBDUE extends graphs one vertex at a time. The extended parents are called children. They consider only best beam width children. It seeks subgraphs to minimize G to DL(D/G) + DL(G). After children are considered, they become the new parents and the process starts over. It will only repeat this process limit number of times or until there is nothing left to consider. Finally, the most frequent sub graph is returned.

*   **[H] Input:** A graph G, a database D, the beam search width beam width and a limit on the depth first search.
*   **Output:** The set of frequent subgraph S which contain max best or fewer sub-graphs.

parentsallsinglevertexsubgraphsinD search depth()

Sφ search depth < limitandparents ≠| φ parents Generate children *ofthebeam widthbestchildren*

the beam_width best children search depth search_depth + 1 **return**S
The results of SUBDUE are as follows:

1. **Positive Graphs:** 8054 vertices, 16113 edges, 229632 bits (input provided is 1 graph, 8054 are the vertices and 16113 are the edges con- necting the above-mentioned vertices).
2. Unique labels (labels of vertices and edges which are not repeated in first iteration)

1 initial substructures
(1st iteration)
Best 3 substructures:

- **Substructure:** value = 1.01068, pos instances = 626, neg instances = 0
  ○ Graph(2, 2e):
    ▪ v 1 node
    ▪ v 2 node
    ▪ u 1 1 edges
    ▪ u 1 2 edges

(most frequently occurring substructure in the graph and value of substruc-ture is calculated using DL(G)/(DL(G/S)+DL(S)), where standard encod-ing bits are 8, 8 and 4 for vertex, edge and pointer):

- **Substructure:** Value = 0.992782, pos instances = 833, neg instances = 0 Graph(2v,1e):
  ○ v 1 node
  ○ v 2 node
  ○ u 1 2 edges
- **Substructure:** Value = 0.987433, pos instances = 378, neg instances = 0 Graph(2v,3e):
  ○ v 1 node
  ○ v 2 node
  ○ u 2 2 edges
  ○ u 2 2 edges
  ○ u 2 1 edges

Elapsed time for iteration 1 = 30 seconds. (time taken to complete first iteration)

Cluster Analysis

Cluster analysis is the art of finding groups in the data. It involves building groups known as clusters. Cluster is a collection of data objects similar to one another within the same cluster, dissimilar to the objects in other clusters. Classification of similar objects into the same group is an important activity because it adds more meaning to the data and will become useful information for analysis. The data is read and represented in the form of a graph that forms as the input for the methods of cluster analysis. A graph G is a set of vertices (nodes) known by v connected by edges (links) known by e. Thus G = (v, e) which means to say that a graph consists of edges and vertices. An edge is a link between two nodes. The edges form relations among the vertices. Based on the relations, the similarity among the nodes can be obtained and using this measure the nodes can be grouped to form a cluster. A cluster can also be called community; it refers to a group of nodes having denser relations with each other than with the rest of the network. A wide range of methods are used to reveal clusters in a network. This analysis involves analysis of clusters of a data set using four methods of graph cluster analysis (Hu, Wang & Xu, 2012).

K-Spanning Tree Clustering Technique

The data set used for K-spanning tree consists of interactions represented by the edges among the developers with a weighted value for each edge. The algorithm obtains the Minimum Spanning Tree (MST) or minimum weight spanning tree of input graph G of the data set using the PRIM's algorithm. Given a connected, undirected graph, a spanning tree of that graph is a subgraph that is a tree and connects all the vertices together. A single graph can have many different spanning trees. A minimum spanning tree (MST) is then a spanning tree with weight less than the weight of every other spanning tree. The PRIM's algorithm selects a random vertex from the input graph and connects it to the other vertices by choosing the edge with the minimum weighted value. It follows the same principle until the last vertex of the graph is traversed. The minimum spanning tree obtained from PRIM's algorithm is used as the input for the K-spanning tree algorithm. A threshold is specified for the number of clusters required, denoted as k. From the input graph obtained from PRIM's algorithm k-1 edges with highest weightage values are removed. This results in clusters being formed.

- **Input:** $G(V, E)$, K
- **Output:** K number of Clusters
  - **Step 1:** Applying $P RIM'S$ algorithm to get minimum spanning tree:

$P (V, E) PRIMS(G(V, E))$

  - **Step 2:** Removing $K - 1$ Highest Weighted edges from $P (V, E)$.
  - **Step 3:** $C\{C_1...C_k\}K$ clusters formed from Step 2.

Highly Connected Subgraphs Clustering Technique

This algorithm was published by Erez Hartuv and Ron Shamir in 1999. The input graph is converted into several clusters that are said to be highly connected. A cluster is said to be highly connected if the number of edges formed by the sub-graph representing the cluster is greater than half the number of vertices in that cluster. This condition suffices that every node in the cluster will have at least one common neighbour with other nodes. The set of edges whose removal disconnects a graph is called a cut. The cut is performed on the graph depending on the input specified. A cluster

Figure 4. Minimal spanning tree for 5 nodes

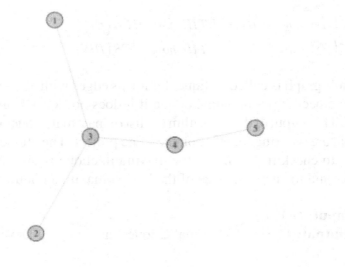

Figure 5. Clusters formed after cutting k-1 highest weighted edges

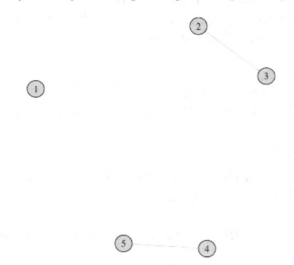

is formed only if the said condition is met. In this algorithm, CUT specifies the threshold to be used so that after cutting off the specified edges, a set of sub-graphs are obtained. For each of the sub-graphs only if the number of edges are greater than the half of the count of vertices, it will be considered as a highly connected sub-graph, $k(H_i)$ represents the edges in the sub-graph (H_i). Otherwise, the process is repeated again.

- **Input:** $G(V, E)$, t
- **Output:** *RESULT*

$$i \le tK\left(Hi\right) > n\ /\ 2\ RESULTHi\ goto\ HCS\left(Hi\right)$$
$$i \le tK\left(Hi\right) > n\ /\ 2\ RESULTHi\ goto\ HCS\left(Hi\right)$$

A sub-graph is called a clique if it forms edges with all the pairs of nodes. A clique becomes a maximal clique if it does not form a subset of a bigger clique. The output of the algorithm is a list of maximal cliques of the developer IDs that are working together on the same project. The clique problems dealt with is to check if the size of the maximum clique is bigger than the given data set and to check the size of the largest maximal clique.

- **Input:** $G(V, E)$
- **Output:** C, Set of Maximal Cliques involving all Developers

$C = \{\varnothing\}$

v in V of $G(V, E)$ find a clique c with vertex v

remove all edges in c from G

add c to C

Betweenness Centrality

Betweenness centrality quantifies the degree to which a vertex or edge occurs on the shortest path between all the other pairs of nodes. It helps to get the more precise rank of the developers. It has two variations

- Vertex betweenness
- Edge betweenness

1. **Vertex Betweenness:** The number of shortest paths in the graph G that passthrough a given node. The centrality of each node is calculated using the degree count of the nodes. The highest centrality measured node will be identified and the graph will be split. This process is iterative. Clusters are formed until the centrality measure of the highest node in the cluster is less than the specified centrality threshold.
2. **Edge Betweenness:** The number of shortest paths in the graph G that pass through given edge. The centrality is calculated for every edge based on the betweenness in the graph. The process is similar to the vertex betweenness clustering.

Data Set

The data set used is homogeneous. For the K-spanning tree clustering technique the data set consists of edges formed by the developer IDs and the weightage of the edges. The edges of the data set indicate that the developers are working together on a project. The weight of the edge represents the completion of the project by the developers of that edge. The number of edges in the data set is 33344 and the developers in the data set is 22376.

For the the rest of the methods, the data set used contains only the edges between the developers, no weights representing the edges. Likewise, the edges represent the developers working on the same project. The number of edges in the data set is 11714 the number of nodes in the data set is 11496.

Analysis Performed on the Methods of Graph Cluster Analysis

The only parameter given is the degree of the vertices. The only exception is K-spanning tree algorithm which uses data set along with weights because of the usage of PRIM's algorithm which produces a minimum spanning tree. The remaining methods use a data set without weighted values for the edges. Using the degree count of the vertex more information has to be generated regarding the data set. The various information that could be generated using the graph cluster methods are the number of developers in the data set, the number of clusters formed, the minimum number of developers in the cluster, the maximum number of developers in the cluster, the average number of developers in the cluster.

The average number of developers in a cluster can be calculated for only those methods where the developer IDs don't repeat themselves in more than one cluster. The reason being that the count of the items in all the clusters greatly exceeds the value of the total number of developers of the data set. Among the methods that are used, average number of developers can be calculated for K-spanning tree clustering techniques, highly connected subgraph clustering and edge betweenness variation of the centrality betweenness clustering technique. The other methods namely maximal clique enumeration and vertex betweenness techniques have repeated developer IDs in the clusters that get formed, hence the average number of developers in a cluster cannot be calculated.

The above-mentioned details provide the insights with respect to the raw data set which had only undirected degree count of the vertices. The clustering process should also be evaluated to check for the performance. Hence, the purity of clustering is checked. Unfortunately, this measure can only to be used on a method where the average number of developers in a cluster can be calculated. The value of purity of clustering will be in the range of 0-1. Value closer to 1 ensures good clustering and vice versa for the the values closer to 0.

For the methods where purity of clustering cannot be calculated, the cohesion between every pair of vertex can be calculated. There are major disadvantages to perform this measure:

- Time complexity is very high.
- Does not produce a great deal of information.

Results

Results of HCS Clustering

Total No of developers in the dataset = 11496 Total No of clusters formed = 3668

Minimum No of developers in a cluster = 1 Maximum No of developers in a cluster = 8 Average No of Developers in a cluster = 3.13 No of cuts specified is = 3

Number of clusters with average number of developers = 946 Purity of the clustering algorithm = 0.341

The variation between the maximum number of developers and minimum number of developers in a cluster is low and hence its purity value is better than the other algorithms. The clusters are formed with developers only if a developer has a mutual friend with all the other developers in the cluster.

Results of K-Span Clustering

Total No of developers in the dataset = 22376 Total No of clusters formed = 4005

Cluster with maximum No of developer = 8925 Cluster with minimum No of developers =1 Average No of developers forming cluster = 5.58701

The clusters with average number of developers = 70 Purity of the clustering algorithm = 0.01765

The K cuts are made on the minimal traversal tree. K specified is 4, 3 edges with highest weight are cut. The highest weighted edges are repeated between many vertices; therefore, all the edges that are the highest 3 in this case regardless of being repeated will be cut off. The variation between the maximum developers in a cluster and minimum developers in a cluster is big. Hence, the purity of this algorithm is very low.

Results of Maximal Clique Enumeration

Total No of developers in the dataset = 11496 Total No of cliques formed = 10138

Minimum No of developers in a clique = 2 Maximum No of developers in a clique = 5

The average no of developers in a clique cannot be found because the developers repeat themselves in different cliques. All the maximal cliques formed are unique, ie; the same set of developers in one clique are not repeated in another clique. The developer with id 100 is participating in most of the maximal cliques with other developers to form unique cliques and from this statement it can inferred that developer with id 100 is participating in several projects in comparison to others.

Results of Vertex Betweenness

Total No of developers in the dataset = 11496 Total No of clusters formed = 6334

Minimum No of Developers in a cluster = 2 Maximum No of Developers in a cluster = 49

The threshold used is 0.2 which means that a cluster will be formed only if the highest centrality in the cluster corresponding to a developer is less than the threshold. The developers are repeated so the average number of developers cannot be found.

Results of Edge Betweenness

Total No of developers in the dataset = 11496 Total No of clusters formed = 984

Minimum No of developers in a cluster = 2 Maximum No of Developers in a cluster = 8927

Average No of Developers in a cluster = 12.76 Clusters with average number of developers = 4 Purity of the clustering algorithm = 0.00408163

The threshold used is 0.2 which means that a cluster will be formed only if the centrality in the cluster corresponding to a pair of developers is less than the threshold. The developers are not repeated hence the average number of developers working on a project together can be found. The variation between the clusters containing maximum and minimum developers is large hence the purity is very low. Purity of a cluster is inversely proportional to the variation between the maximum and the minimum clusters containing the developers.

CONCLUSION

The main concern in SNA is analysing the interactions within a social network to gain more knowledge and to retrive hidden information from it. Influence Spotting in the Network is effectively analysed using PageRank algorithm and most influential nodes of the Network are found. Link Prediction Algorithm is applied using different Proximity measures and concluded that Correlation measure gives the better accuracy to the developer-developer relation dataset. Frequent Subgraph Mining is done using SUBDUE Algorithm and the whole network is analysed for the frequent subgraphs. Clustering is done using HCS, K-Span, Max- imal Clique and Betweenness Centrality techniques to gain more insights such as average number of developers working together, maximum number of develop- ers working together, minimum number of developers working together. Graph Mining techniques used here aims at deriving useful information from the dataset containing very basic interactions among developers. Analysing such data for more Information like the top active developers in the entire network, predicting the possible interests of the developers based on their history, grouping the developers together to analyse betweenness and to find the groups with similar interests using subgraphs mining for more accurate results drives the main idea behind the whole analysis. The main goal is to apply novel techniques to improve the performance of the algorithms for real time data.

REFERENCES

Borgatti, S. P., Mehra, A., Brass, D. J., & Labianca, G. (2009). Network analysis in the social sciences. *Science*, *323*(5916), 892–895. doi:10.1126/science.1165821 PMID:19213908

Carrington, P. J., Scott, J., & Wasserman, S. (2005). Models and methods in social network analysis. Cambridge University Press. doi:10.1017/CBO9780511811395

Cheng-Hao, C., Wan-Chuen, W., Cheng-Chi, W., Tzung-Shi, C., & Jen-Jee, C. (2013). Friend recommendation for location-based mobile social networks. In *Proceedings of the 2013 Seventh International Conference on Innovative Mobile and Internet Services in Ubiquitous Computing (IMIS)* (pp. 365–370). IEEE.

Fire, M., Tenenboim, L., Lesser, O., Puzis, R., Rokach, L., & Elovici, Y. (2011). Link prediction in social networks using computationally efficient topological features. In *Proceedings of the 2011 IEEE third international conference on Privacy, security, risk and trust (passat) and 2011 IEEE third international conference on social computing (Socialcom)* (pp. 73–80). IEEE.

Hu, Z., Wang, X., & Xu, K. (2012). Mining community in social network using call detail records. In *Proceedings of the 2012 9th International Conference on Fuzzy Systems and Knowledge Discovery (FSKD)* (pp. 1641–1645). IEEE. doi:10.1109/FSKD.2012.6233712

Jain, A., Sharma, R., Dixit, G., & Tomar, V. (2013). Page ranking algorithms in web mining, limitations of existing methods and a new method for indexing web pages. In *Proceedings of the 2013 International Conference on Communication Systems and Network Technologies (CSNT)* (pp. 640–645). IEEE.

Jamali, M., & Abolhassani, H. (2006). Different aspects of social network analysis. In *Proceedings of the IEEE/WIC/ACM International Conference on Web Intelligence WI '06* (pp. 66–72). IEEE.

Kimura, M., Yamakawa, K., Saito, K., & Motoda, H. (2008). Community analysis of influential nodes for information diffusion on a social network. In *Proceedings of the IEEE International Joint Conference on Neural Networks IJCNN '08* (pp. 1358–1363). IEEE.

Kuramochi, M., & Karypis, G. (2001). Frequent subgraph discovery. In *Proceedings of the IEEE International Conference on Data Mining ICDM '01* (pp. 313–320). IEEE. doi:10.1109/ICDM.2001.989534

Liben-Nowell, D., & Kleinberg, J. (2007). The link-prediction problem for social networks. *Journal of the American Society for Information Science and Technology, 58*(7), 1019–1031. doi:10.1002/asi.20591

Lim, S. L., Quercia, D., & Finkelstein, A. (2010). Stakenet: using social networks to analyse the stakeholders of large-scale software projects. In *Proceedings of the 32nd ACM/IEEE International Conference on Soft- ware Engineering* (Vol. 1, pp. 295–304). ACM. doi:10.1145/1806799.1806844

Murata, T., & Moriyasu, S. (2007). Link prediction of social networks based on weighted proximity measures. In *Proceedings of the IEEE/WIC/ACM International Conference on Web Intelligence* (pp. 85–88). IEEE. doi:10.1109/WI.2007.52

Nijssen, S., & Kok, J. N. (2005). The gaston tool for frequent subgraph mining. *Electronic Notes in Theoretical Computer Science, 127*(1), 77–87. doi:10.1016/j.entcs.2004.12.039

Nowell, D. L., & Kleinberg, J. (2003). The link prediction problem for social networks. In *Proceedings of the 12ᵗʰ International Conference on Information and Knowledge Management year* (pp. 556-559). Academic Press.

Pan, L. (2007). *Effective and efficient methodologies for social network analysis* (PhD thesis).

Seo, S. W., Kyong, J., & Eun-Jin, I. (2012). Social network analysis algorithm on a many-core gpu. In *Proceedings of the 2012 Fourth International Conference on Ubiquitous and Future Networks (ICUFN)* (pp. 217–218). IEEE.

Thi, D. B., & Hoang, T. A. N. (2013). Features extraction for link prediction in social networks. In *Proceedings of the 2013 13th International Conference on Computational Science and Its Applications (ICCSA)* (pp. 192–195). IEEE.

Thomas, L. T., Valluri, S. R., & Karlapalem, K. (2006). Margin: Maximal frequent subgraph mining. In *Proceedings of the Sixth International Conference on Data Mining ICDM '06* (pp. 1097–1101). IEEE.

Chapter 8

A Multi-Step Process Towards Integrating Free and Open Source Software in Engineering Education

ABSTRACT

Free and Open Source Software (FOSS) is a phenomenon which has overgrown its software origins. From being viewed as a cheaper software alternative, it has become a fountain head of ideas which are adopted cheerfully by people across many domains. From a collaborative effort to build world's biggest encyclopaedia to artists sharing their works under liberal licences, FOSS has become a reference for global, peer-reviewed, volunteer based production model of creating knowledge commons. With everyone from governments to big corporates displaying keen interest in FOSS, it is high time educationalists too take FOSS into classrooms. The ecology of FOSS is filled with more than just a set of software from which a teacher can choose from. He can bring the rich set of coding practices, licensing options, production model and importantly a different world-view by adopting FOSS in teaching. The benefits for students too are many ranging from using modern tools to participating in real world software development. There are many scholarly papers reporting the innovative use of FOSS in teaching graduate courses. By combining these studies with our experience of delivering courses in FOSS, we present a three-stage process which can be adopted by teachers and institutes to utilise the benefits of FOSS to the fullest.

DOI: 10.4018/978-1-5225-3707-6.ch008

INTRODUCTION

The freedoms provided to users by Free Software have their roots in academic culture (Foltin et al., 2011). Education system has a long history of practices like distributed development, peer review and revision based on feedback which are also found in FOSS and therefore education sector is but the natural home for FOSS (Carmichael & Honour, 2002). FOSS is attractive to educators because as scientists they are used to share and allow others to modify their ideas (O'Hara & Kay, 2003). Just like scientists are interested in various phenomenons for the case of curiosity, FOSS developers too get involved in projects that interest them. While scientists share their results publicly, FOSS developers too share the source code (Bezroukov, 1999). So, FOSS should be the natural choice of educators.

The utilitarian idea of teaching is often reflected upon and a writer comments it is strange to convince educators that it is good to share information. Educators should use FOSS because software industry discriminates access to software on economic grounds.

As software forms important part of knowledge in modern age, it should not be allowed to be dominated by commercial players. Hence using FOSS becomes not merely an economic but moral obligation for teachers (Hart, 2003).

Figure 1. The process of integration FOSS in education

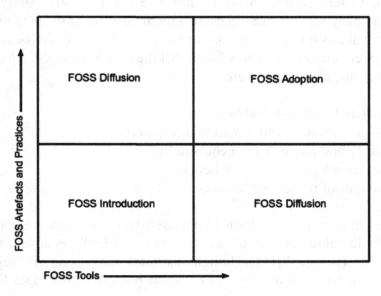

141

There is rich literature available on why and how of FOSS usage in educational institutes. UNDP published a primer on FOSS in education discussing various issues like the potential benefits of using FOSS, various FOSS tools for common academic and administrative usage and legal issues which should be considered while switching over to FOSS (Tong, 2004). But introducing FOSS in institutes can be long and daunting experience for educators as there is FUD (Fear, Uncertainty and Doubt) surrounding FOSS usage. Therefore, we propose a three step process for integrating FOSS in education system. We focus on Engineering education as we are involved in this sector but we hope this approach can be customised to other domains as well. The process is depicted in Figure 1 and is detailed in the following sections.

Stage 1: FOSS Introduction

FOSS is making its presence felt in education sectors of developed countries. In UK, 38% of higher education reported that their institutions have an IT strategy which explicitly considers FOSS (Attwell, 2005). 57% of higher education sector in US use FOSS products (Abel, 2006). But some advanced nations and many developing nations are yet to identify the advantage FOSS brings to education system. A study reported that it is highly unlikely that a wide adoption of FOSS to replace incumbent systems will sweep through educational institutions in emerging markets like India, Brazil, Russia, South Africa, and China (Gangadharan & Butler, 2012). In another study, it was found that many schools in Sweden also seem unaware of the potential with FOSS as enablers for innovative use of IT (Lundell & Gamalielsson, 2013).

In a systematic review, it was found that the drivers of FOSS adoption in US higher education sector were:

1. Social and philosophical benefits;
2. Software development methodology benefits;
3. Security and risk management benefits;
4. Software adoption life cycle benefits;
5. Total cost of ownership benefits (Rooij, 2009).

While educators are attracted to FOSS due to increased student engagement and active learning support, administrators love FOSS because it reduces licence fees (Rooij, 2011). Though institutes have concerns regarding security, support and longevity of FOSS, the potential advantages like cost reduction and vendor independence help matters turn towards FOSS (Rooij, 2007). In addition to providing the possibility of using different tools, the definite advantage of FOSS in education is that it allows innovation. With the availability of open content and open standards, it is possible for educators to experiment with different pedagogic applications (Attwell, 2005).

These and many such reports prompt us to suggest that the first step regarding FOSS usage in classroom should be to provide holistic introduction of FOSS to students. That is because first, many countries are yet to understand the potential of FOSS and second, even if they are using FOSS they do it mainly for technical and economic reasons. This limits the discussion of FOSS as a cheaper alternative and hides the moral and ethical urgency of embracing FOSS. Also, educators cannot be blind to the increasing commercialisation of every aspect of software which hinders the growth and reach of knowledge in digital world. FOSS has the potential to bridge the digital divide (Krogh & Spaeth, 2007) and therefore it is necessary to use FOSS in education.

More specifically, we recommend that in addition to encouraging the usage of FOSS tools, it is necessary that they are aware of its history and culture. Bringing in the narratives of FOSS heroes like Richard M Stallman and Linus Torvalds will help students absorb the spirit of FOSS. They will appreciate Wikipedia more if they learn the collaborative nature of its development. The philosophy of Unix and the ethics of hackers will lay solid foundation to the increased usage and ultimately contribution to FOSS movement. Otherwise students will treat FOSS as just another tool with same or maybe better quality than its counterparts.

Stage 2: FOSS Diffusion

The real advantage of FOSS in education sector is beyond its role as a supplier of development and application tools for students. It can play a constructive role in transforming the teaching methods through what has been identified by pedagogues as 'active learning' (Howison, Conklin & Ossmole, 2005). We propose that the next stage of using FOSS in curriculum should focus on utilising the FOSS artefacts and FOSS practices.

Since FOSS development is a public affair, the entire data covering the lifecycle of software development is now freely available. Educators should bring these valuable resources into classroom so that students get to know how software is created in the real world. For example, FOSS repositories like Sourceforge (Slashdot Media, 2017) and Freecode (Slashdot Media, 2015) give away development data about the software hosted by them including the communication trails. There are also aggregated project data available through projects like FLOSSMOLE (Howison, Conklin & Crowston, 2006). These data can be used to bring qualitative difference in teaching many courses.

In Elon University, USA, FLOSSMOLE data was used in Database course to give real time experience to students. It was also used in Management Information System course to evaluate FOSS projects using established quality methods like Business Readiness Rating (BRR). FLOSSMOLE data was also used in Artificial Intelligence courses to parse the project details using Natural Language Programming techniques (Squire & Duvall, 2009). Linux source code can be used to deliver Operating System course in a better way. The large data sets are ideal to be used in Database and Data Mining course. Availability of source code will help teachers to explain the concepts by 'dissecting' the real projects and teach the 'software anatomy'.

Software Engineering educators are always in search of relevant materials and novel pedagogies that will provide life-long learning experiences and improve the quality of students learning outcomes (Sowe, Stamelos & Deligiannis, 2006). FOSS is both interesting and intriguing from Software Engineering perspective. At first, the practices followed in its development seem to contradict the established norms prescribed in software engineering textbooks. But a careful study will reveal that the differences are just superficial. Increasingly many educators have used FOSS in interesting ways to deliver Software Engineering courses. In the context of increased use of FOSS components in modern software, there are attempts to reorient the Software Engineering education to help students acquire the required skills (Hawthorne & Perry, 2006). In Aristotle University, Greece, students used the real projects hosted in Sourceforge in Software Testing course. They found bugs, reported them to the community and got a first-hand experience of real time quality assurance procedures (Sowe, Stamelos & Deligiannis, 2006). At the University of Skvde, students were first involved in contributing to Wikipedia to understand collaborative development model. Then they selected a FOSS project to participate. They were not only making code commits or fix bugs, but were encouraged to write design documents and help manuals (Lundell, Persson & Lings, 2007). In Western Oregon University and Oregon State University, USA, students were asked to join and contribute to FOSS projects (Morgan & Jensen, 2014).

But joining a FOSS project directly and start contributing may be difficult for many students because each project follows its own unique practice and tools. Therefore, in Tampere University of Technology, educators developed a reputation model and a concrete reputation environment known as KommGame that mimics real FOSS projects (Goduguluri, Kilamo & Hammouda, 2011). Based on our experience in similar attempts, we highly recommend that students be hand-held in initial stages by using controlled environment like this one.

FOSS projects allow students to contribute to an ethical and worthwhile cause in addition to learning good practices of global software development models. University of Lincoln identified the One Laptop Per Child (OLPC) project as a potentially excellent way of getting students involved in collaborative software development (Boldyreff, Capiluppi, Knowles et al., 2009). The Humanitarian FOSS project across multiple universities is an example of successful use of FOSS in education system. The faculty members involved in these projects underlined the importance of sensitising the students regarding the philosophical and ethical roots of FOSS which helped them attract more students to their works (Morelli, Tucker, Danner et al., 2009). In another case, a popular FOSS disaster management solution, Sahana, was used as a basis of teaching Software Engineering course. It is reported that students were highly motivated towards contributing for humanitarian project (Ellis, Morelli, Lanerolle et al., 2007). In Norway, students combined contribution to FOSS projects and doing empirical research regarding the same (Jaccheri & Osterlie, 2007).

Therefore, in FOSS Diffusion stage teachers should first use FOSS artefacts beyond software to bring qualitative difference in various courses. Details regarding code commits, bug lifecycle, software release and communication trails will help students relate their learning to real world. Later students should be introduced to the practices involved in FOSS development such as community collaboration, peer review, and co-creation by making them participate in real projects through careful handholding (Goduguluri, Kilamo & Hammouda, 2011). Not only will this help students gain more knowledge through active participation but it also potentially helps ensure FOSS communities have enough qualified developers to draw from to meet their needs (Morgan & Jensen, 2014).

Stage 3: FOSS Adoption

After the students are familiar with the FOSS philosophy, tools and practices teachers can start offering a separate course in this topic. More than a decade of research in FOSS has resulted in a rich body of knowledge. Multiple taxonomies are also proposed which signal the maturity of the field. With the availability of books which capture multiple aspects of FOSS, teachers have enough resources to deliver the course. More importantly FOSS presents an interesting premise which deserves a thorough investigation by academic community.

There are multiple reports of universities offering stand alone course covering various issues in FOSS. Most of these courses focus just on single dimension like development practices, legal issues like IPR or specific FOSS tools. As discussed in previous sections, it is futile if students are not introduced to ethical and moral issues regarding FOSS. It is also necessary that they study the unique development process, legal issues encountered in using FOSS and the potential areas where FOSS can bring effective changes. To address these issues, we had offered a course titled 'Free and Open Source Software Engineering' to graduate students whose details are as follows

Overview of the Subject

The subject covered the vast expanse of FOSS by critically examining five issues:

1. What conditions led to the emergence of FOSS?
2. What motivates volunteers to contribute to FOSS?
3. What are the Software Engineering processes followed in FOSS?
4. How can FOSS be used effectively in public administration, business, education, and research?
5. What are the legal and economic issues surrounding the usage of FOSS?

Text Books

1. Steve Weber, *The Success of Open Source*, Harvard University Press, 2004.
2. Joseph Feller et al. (Eds.), *Perspectives on Free and Open Source Software*, MIT Press, 2005.

Delivery Model

Classroom lectures coupled with open discussions based on documentaries, telefilms and docu-dramas covering various issues of FOSS.

Videos of all lectures are available at http://goo.gl/ciZJlR.

Innovations in Teaching

1. Usage of e-learn tool for collaboration.
2. Inclusion of videos in course materials.
3. Open discussions covering many interesting topics.
4. Mandatory reading exercises.
5. Encouragement to community service.

Evaluation Methods

In addition to tests and book reviews, community participation activities were also considered for evaluation. This gave enough scope for students to display their learning abilities.

Feedback From Students

For many students, this was the first exposure to FOSS. They responded positively to the course and many said they would continue to use and contribute to FOSS.

Many universities have started offering master degrees in FOSS. Though there are no such attempts in English speaking countries, Spain, Portugal, Italy, Colombia, Equadar and Mexico grant post graduate master degrees in FOSS (Leon, Robles, Gonzalez-Barahona et al., 2014). We suggest that universities in India too look at this possibility as there is increasing demand for people who can work in a globally collaborative environment which can be better taught through FOSS. The paradigm shift in the software development methods and tools are well internalised by FOSS projects. Increasingly corporates too are getting involved in FOSS development and governance. Therefore, the stage is set for offering full fledged degree in this domain.

CONCLUSION

We propose a three-stage process which will help educators and institutes to reduce the risks and increase the benefits of using FOSS. In first stage teachers should move beyond treating FOSS just as another tool and sensitise students regarding the history, philosophy, legal and economic issues of FOSS.

In next stage, they should use FOSS artefacts beyond software in delivering courses like Databases and Operating System. Software Engineering teaching should be reoriented to include FOSS practices so that students learn from participating in real projects. In stage three institutes can offer stand alone courses and later start master's degree programs in FOSS.

REFERENCES

Attwell, G. (2005). What is the significance of open source software for the education and training community. In *Proceedings of the First International Conference on Open Source Systems (OSS 2005)*, Genova, Italy, July 11.

Bezroukov, N. (1999). Open source software development as a special type of academic research: Critique of vulgar raymondism. *First Monday*, *4*(10), 1999. doi:10.5210/fm.v4i10.696

Boldyreff, C., Capiluppi, A., Knowles, T., & Munro, J. (2009). Undergraduate research opportunities in oss. In Open Source Ecosystems: Diverse Communities Interacting (pp. 340–350). Springer.

Carmichael, P., & Honour, L. (2002). Open source as appropriate technology for global education. *International Journal of Educational Development*, *22*(1), 47–53. doi:10.1016/S0738-0593(00)00077-8

Ellis, H. J. C., Morelli, R. A., Lanerolle, T. R. D., & Hislop, G. W. (2007). Holistic software engineering education based on a humanitarian open source project. In *Proceedings of the 20th Conference on Software Engineering Education & Training CSEET'07* (pp. 327–335). IEEE.

Foltin, M., Fodrek, P., Blaho, M., & Murgaˇs, J. (2011). Open source technologies in education. In *Recent Researches in Educational Technologies: Proceedings of the 8th WSEAS International Conference on Engineering Education (EDUCATION'11)* (pp. 131–135).

Gangadharan, G. R., & Butler, M. (2012). Free and open source software adoption in emerging markets: An empirical study in the education sector. In Open Source Systems: Long-Term Sustainability (pp. 244–249). Springer.

Goduguluri, V., Kilamo, T., & Hammouda, I. (2011). Kommgame: A reputation environment for teaching open source software. In Open Source Systems: Grounding Research (pp. 312–315). Springer.

Hart, T.D. (2003). Open source in education.

Hawthorne, M. J., & Perry, D. E. (2006). Software engineering education in the era of outsourcing, distributed development, and open source software: challenges and opportunities. In *Software Engineering Education in the Modern Age* (pp. 166–185). Springer. doi:10.1007/11949374_11

Howison, J., Conklin, M., & Crowston, K. (2006). Flossmole: A collaborative repository for floss research data and analyses. *International Journal of Information Technology and Web Engineering*, *1*(3), 17–26. doi:10.4018/jitwe.2006070102

Howison, J., Conklin, M., & Ossmole, K. C. (2005). A collaborative repository for floss research data and analyses. In *Proceedings of the First International Conference on Open Source Systems*, Genova.

Jaccheri, L., & Osterlie, T. (2007). Open source software: a source of possibilities for software engineering education and empirical software engineering. In *Proceedings of the First International Workshop on Emerging Trends in FLOSS Research and Development FLOSS'07* (p. 5). IEEE.

Krogh, G., & Spaeth, S. (2007). The open source software phenomenon: Characteristics that promote research. *The Journal of Strategic Information Systems*, *16*(3), 236–253. doi:10.1016/j.jsis.2007.06.001

Leon, S. R. M., Robles, G., Gonzalez-Barahona, J. M. (2014). Considerations regarding the creation of a post-graduate master's degree in free software. In Open Source Software: Mobile Open Source Technologies (pp. 123–132). Springer.

Lundell, B., & Gamalielsson, J. (2013). Open standards and open source in swedish schools: On promotion of openness and transparency. In Open Source Software: Quality Verification (pp. 207–221). Springer.

Lundell, B., Persson, A., & Lings, B. (2007). Learning through practical involvement in the oss ecosystem: Experiences from a master's assignment. In Open Source Development, Adoption and Innovation (pp. 289–294). Springer.

Morelli, R., Tucker, A., Danner, N., Lanerolle, T. R. D., Ellis, H. J. C., Izmirli, O., & Parker, G. et al. (2009). Revitalizing computing education through free and open source software for humanity. *Communications of the ACM*, *52*(8), 67–75. doi:10.1145/1536616.1536635

Morgan, B., & Jensen, C. (2014). Lessons learned from teaching open source software development. In Open Source Software: Mobile Open Source Technologies (pp. 133–142). Springer.

O'Hara, K. J., & Kay, J. S. (2003). Open source software and computer science education. *Journal of Computing Sciences in Colleges*, *18*(3), 1–7.

Rooij, S. W. (2007). Perceptions of open source versus commercial software: Is higher education still on the fence? *Journal of Research on Technology in Education*, *39*(4), 433–453. doi:10.1080/15391523.2007.10782491

Slashdot Media. (2015). Welcome to Freecode. Retrieved March 12, 2017, from http://freecode.com/

Slashdot Media. (2017). Find, Create, and Publish Open Source software for free. Retrieved March 12, 2017, from http://sourceforge.net/

Sowe, S. K., Stamelos, I., & Deligiannis, I. (2006). A framework for teaching software testing using foss methodology. In *Open Source Systems* (pp. 261–266). Springer. doi:10.1007/0-387-34226-5_26

Squire, M., & Duvall, S. (2009). Using floss project metadata in the undergraduate classroom. In Open Source Ecosystems: Diverse Communities Interacting (pp. 330–339). Springer.

Tong, T. W. (2004). *Free/open source software education*. Malaysia: United Nations Development Programmes Asia-Pacific Information Programme.

Conclusion

The present work throws some interesting observations regarding the basic premise of FOSS world. The promise of open invitation to the developers which is touted as the single most unique feature of FOSS world, it appears, has not yielded great results. The fact that only 10% of the registered users in Sourceforge.net get themselves affiliated to a project proves that the conversion from interested public to dedicated developers is happening at a very slow rate. The long-term success of the FOSS movement will depend on how effectively this conversion rate is improved.

The ability to attract like minded people and involve them in the development is another popular belief in FOSS world. Eric Raymond said that "Every good work of software starts by scratching a developer's personal itch". Though a developer starts the project alone, it was assumed that over a period of time, other developers will start contributing to the project. But the results from this work shows that nearly one third of the projects in Sourceforge.net have only one developer. The failure of projects to attract more developers may prove to be the single important reason for the death of FOSS projects.

The size of project groups has been an issue in Software Engineering discussions. The data from Top Ranked projects from Sourceforge.net shows that they have a large number of developers. It also shows that nearly one third of the developers in the projects are dedicated to that project. Accordingly, we can conclude that successful FOSS projects display a singular feature of large number of dedicated developers. One of the important contributions of this work is to analyse the nature of developer migration patters. It was important to know whether few developers, who by the virtue of their presence, make a project successful. The present work shows that a successful project contains the right mix of experienced and new developers. Surprisingly, it was found that the number of new developers is slightly higher than experienced developers thereby proving again that FOSS ecology is still open to all.

The decrease in number of tasks that are alloted to developers in Top Ranked project is a clear sign of project maturity. This trend is in line with the popular notion that the product reaches a state of equilibrium after few months of use. The reduction in the number of days required to close an issue further testifies the same fact.

This work contributes to the knowledge and practice of Software Engineering by examining the phenomenon of Free and Open Source Software (FOSS). FOSS has made rapid strides into the IT landscape and enjoys huge popularity in some domains like Operating System (GNU-Linux), Webserver (Apache) and Internet tools (BIND, Sendmail) to name a few. The practices followed in FOSS including open participation, peer review and semi-structured governance models is being applied in many domains beyond software. Wikipedia and its sister projects like Wikibooks, Open Science, Open Governance and Citizen Engineering are examples of applying FOSS development principles. These projects demonstrate that FOSS phenomenon deserves serious attention from researches because though it is being widely applied, very little is known about the forces behind its success.

Proposing a new taxonomy for FOSS research which is refined from an existing work is another contribution of this work. This taxonomy was used to classify the 347 papers presented in OSS conferences from 2005 to 2014. This classification is helpful for two purposes. One it can be used to identify the areas which attract more attention from researchers and two, it can be used to map the evolution of a research area as the papers are listed in chronological order. The major studies in the areas of developer motivation, software development methods, community evolution and quality assurance in FOSS are summarised. This work will enable better understanding of FOSS and identify the common themes of research in this area. Sourceforge.net was selected as a case study for this work as it is one of the largest FOSS repositories hosting more than 300,000 projects. University of Norte Dame provides the data from Sourceforge.net to researchers through a web interface. The data from 2005 to 2013 was considered for the present work. The datasets of 8 years provided enough samples to study the evolution of FOSS ecology. It was found that while projects hosted in Sourceforge.net is steadily increasing over the years, the developers have started to slow down since 2011. The modelling of developer relations as a social network helps visualise the FOSS ecology in a better way. The progressive mapping of developer relations demonstrates the existence of two distinct sets of developers at core and periphery. The core developers seem to be better connected and their cohesiveness may benefit the overall ecology of FOSS because they can share their expertise and enrich the projects they are involved. This phenomenon is also observed in other repositories like Rubyforge and Freecode signalling that this may the natural way people organise in such collaborative networks.

That Sourceforge.net demonstrates power law is not surprising. In any large network, it is natural for newcomers to join popular projects to increase their visibility. This is labelled variously as preferential attachment, rich get richer; follow the crowd and long tail in literature. The large number of projects with single or very small set of developers will have shorter life as the projects will become orphans once the initiator deserts the project and does not hand over the control to anyone else. FOSS ecology has developed a powerful tool to ensure the reincarnation of any dead or inactive project through forking. However, projects with no formal structure and considerable developer base are rarely adopted widely. Very few projects in FOSS ecology succeed and many fail to attract critical mass of developers. How to recruit, train and retain talented developers is a topic which will become important as more corporates become involved in the development and governance of FOSS projects.

The experimental contributions of this work include modelling the Sourceforge.net data as a social network of collaborating developers and studying the resulting structure. The notion of influence is well established in network studies. Selecting a minimum set of nodes who can effectively connect to all the nodes in the network is important for many reasons. In marketing and business network such nodes labelled as 'seed nodes' will be subjects for targeted marketing. In politics, they are called opinion makers and are therefore valued. With social networking emerging in big way in this millennium, this topic has received a renewed interest. In FOSS ecology which involves millions of developers, finding well connected developers becomes challenging. Using different algorithms like Pagerank, High Degree, LDAG, SPS-CELF++ and SimPath, such developers are discovered. What is interesting in these studies is the consistency with which they retain in the top position for many years. This proves that FOSS ecology has a healthy set of dedicated developers who will carry the momentum further.

Applying techniques from Graph Mining to social network created from Sourceforge.net is another major contribution of this work. Extending the theories in data mining to large graphs results in obtaining new perspective about the topic. Given a network of developers, it is possible to find future collaborators using Link Prediction algorithm. This is beneficial for projects to find prospective developers because as discussed earlier, recruiting and retaining critical mass of developers is important for longevity of any project. Mining frequent subgraphs using gSpan and SUBDUE algorithms results in identification of common set of developers who frequently interact with each other. K Spanning and Highly Connected Subgraphs techniques are used to detect the clusters in developer network. Graph mining methods helps in understanding the kind of interactions and collaborations developers have among themselves in Sourceforge.net.

The lessons learnt through study of literature and conduction of experiments is applied in classroom to take the benefits of FOSS to students. The final part of the book records the experience of offering a course in FOSS dealing with issues ranging from its history, development models and areas where FOSS can be effectively used. It further describes a three-stage process to introduce FOSS effectively in Engineering education. The main suggestion of this section is that teachers should not treat FOSS as just a cheaper alternate but introduce its rich philosophy and practices to students. This will help them appreciate FOSS better and turn them into future contributors. Overall this demonstrates how results from labs can be taken to actual field to demonstrate the practical benefits of research work.

The other contributions of the work include development of methods, tools and techniques to manage huge repository of data. With more than 2TB of historical data and 30 to 50 GB of fresh data arriving every month, it was necessary to devise means to store and analyse data in an effective manner. The need to generate graphs involving millions of nodes also required development of novel visualisation methods. Bibilography management also was a challenge as more than 450 works had to be tagged and classified. Overall, this work which aimed to 'study volunteer contributions in the decentralized, globally distributed development models in Free and Open Source Software Engineering' meets its stated objectives and contributes, in a limited way, towards the extension of understanding and application of Free and Open Source Software.

Summarising, with limited scope, the present work contributes to the growing pool of knowledge regarding the development practices followed in FOSS. The results show that even though the FOSS world appears to be working in a chaotic 'bazaar model' on the surface, there is a definite process followed by the developer community. Since the practice followed by FOSS community is different from the traditional software development, there may be some difficulty in understanding them. The world is relying more on software today than anytime before. In such times, these studies will definitely help us to improve our knowledge regarding developing software and enable us to meet our professional obligation of delivering good quality software in right time and price while meeting the user's requirements.

Appendix

ER DIAGRAMS OF RESEARCH DATA

Figure 1. ER diagram of artifact

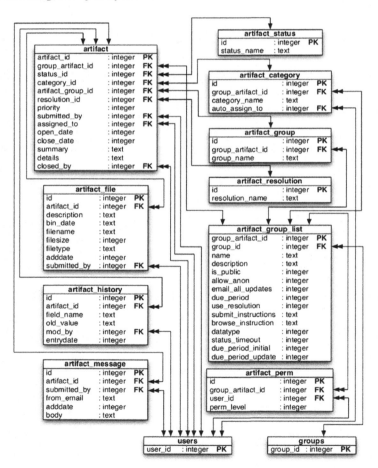

Figure 2. ER diagram of task

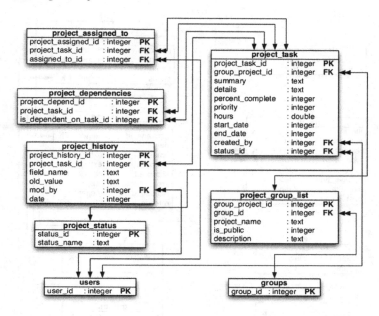

Figure 3. ER diagram of job

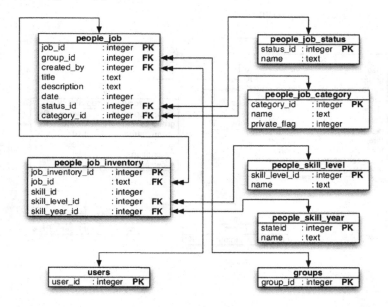

Figure 4. ER diagram of frs

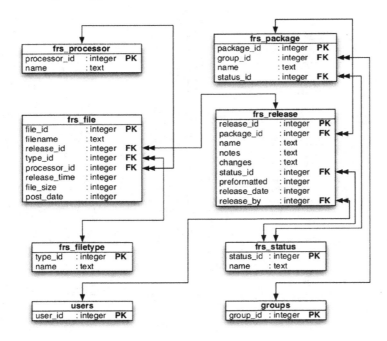

Figure 5. ER diagram of forum

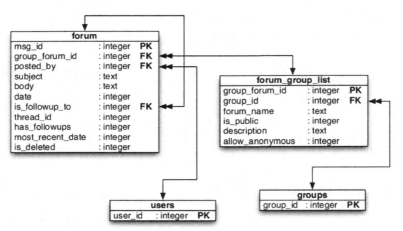

Figure 6. ER diagram of doc

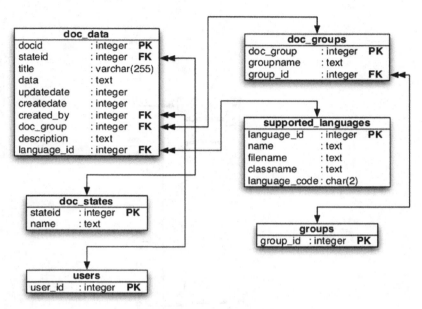

Figure 7. Complete ER diagram: layout

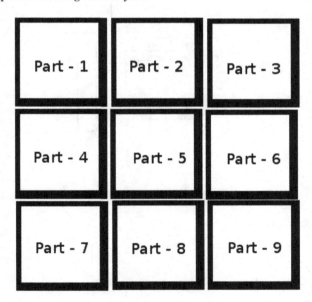

Figure 8. Complete ER diagram: part 1

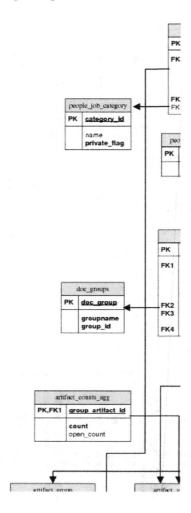

Figure 9. Complete ER diagram: part 2

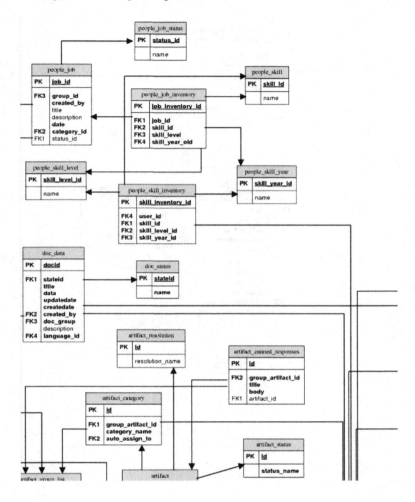

Figure 10. Complete ER diagram: part 3

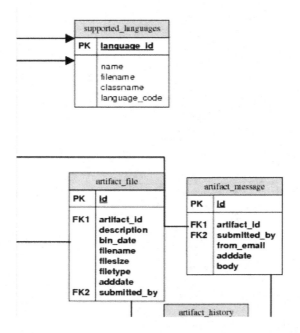

Figure 11. Complete ER diagram: part 4

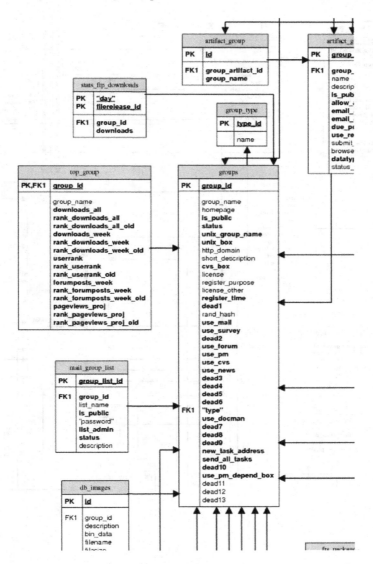

Figure 12. Complete ER diagram: part 5

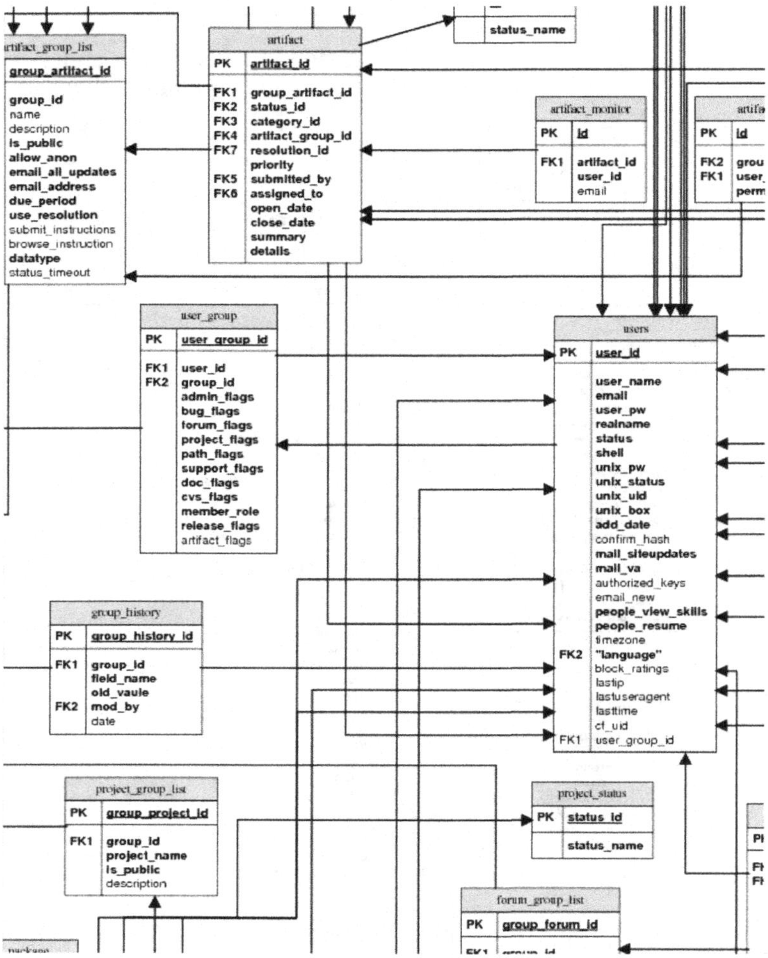

Figure 13. Complete ER diagram: part 6

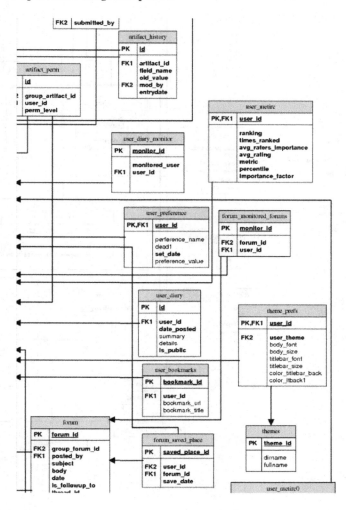

Figure 14. Complete ER diagram: part 7

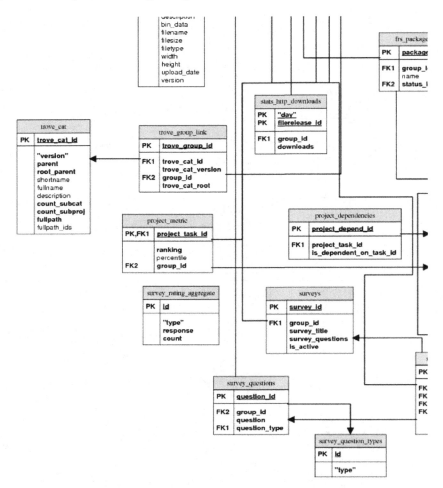

Figure 15. Complete ER diagram: part 8

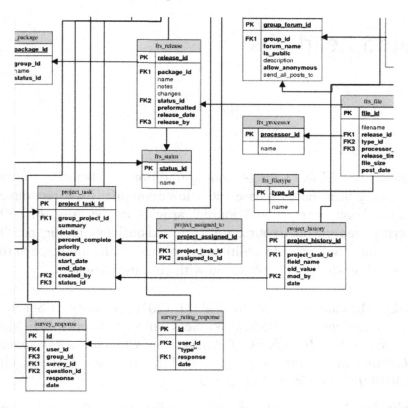

Figure 16. Complete ER diagram: part 9

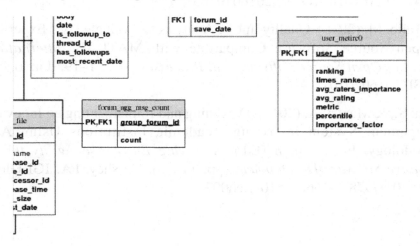

Related Readings

To continue IGI Global's long-standing tradition of advancing innovation through emerging research, please find below a compiled list of recommended IGI Global book chapters and journal articles in the areas of software engineering, free and open source software, and business intelligence. These related readings will provide additional information and guidance to further enrich your knowledge and assist you with your own research.

Abreu, C., Miranda, F., & Mendes, P. M. (2016). Quality of Service and Radio Management in Biomedical Wireless Sensor Networks. In F. Miranda & C. Abreu (Eds.), *Handbook of Research on Computational Simulation and Modeling in Engineering* (pp. 704–725). Hershey, PA: IGI Global. doi:10.4018/978-1-4666-8823-0.ch023

Abu Talib, M. (2016). Open Source Software in the Arab World: A Literature Survey. *International Journal of Open Source Software and Processes*, 7(1), 49–64. doi:10.4018/IJOSSP.2016010103

Abu Talib, M. (2016). Quality in Use Analysis to Evaluate User Experience of Open Source Software Compatible with MATLAB. *International Journal of Open Source Software and Processes*, 7(3), 1–19. doi:10.4018/IJOSSP.2016070101

Ahuja, S., & Mantri, A. (2015). Designing and Implementing an Innovation Management System in Young Academic Institutions Using Agile Methodology. In A. Singh (Ed.), *Achieving Enterprise Agility through Innovative Software Development* (pp. 17–35). Hershey, PA: IGI Global. doi:10.4018/978-1-4666-8510-9.ch002

Al Khawli, T., Eppelt, U., & Schulz, W. (2016). Sensitivity Analysis of Laser Cutting Based on Metamodeling Approach. In F. Miranda & C. Abreu (Eds.), *Handbook of Research on Computational Simulation and Modeling in Engineering* (pp. 618–639). Hershey, PA: IGI Global. doi:10.4018/978-1-4666-8823-0.ch020

Al Shidhani, A., Al Maawali, K., Al Abri, D., & Bourdoucen, H. (2016). A comparative analysis of open source network monitoring tools. *International Journal of Open Source Software and Processes*, 7(2), 1–19. doi:10.4018/IJOSSP.2016040101

Alkkiomäki, V., & Smolander, K. (2015). QSE: Service Elicitation with Qualitative Research Procedures. In V. Díaz, J. Lovelle, & B. García-Bustelo (Eds.), *Handbook of Research on Innovations in Systems and Software Engineering* (pp. 171–185). Hershey, PA: IGI Global. doi:10.4018/978-1-4666-6359-6.ch007

Alves, L. M., Ribeiro, P., & Machado, R. J. (2014). Project-Based Learning: An Environment to Prepare IT Students for an Industry Career. In L. Yu (Ed.), *Overcoming Challenges in Software Engineering Education: Delivering Non-Technical Knowledge and Skills* (pp. 230–249). Hershey, PA: IGI Global. doi:10.4018/978-1-4666-5800-4.ch012

Amrollahi, A., Khansari, M., & Manian, A. (2014). Success of open source in developing countries: the case of Iran. *International Journal of Open Source Software and Processes*, 5(1), 50–65. doi:10.4018/ijossp.2014010103

Angelis, L., Mittas, N., & Chatzipetrou, P. (2015). A Framework of Statistical and Visualization Techniques for Missing Data Analysis in Software Cost Estimation. In V. Díaz, J. Lovelle, & B. García-Bustelo (Eds.), *Handbook of Research on Innovations in Systems and Software Engineering* (pp. 71–97). Hershey, PA: IGI Global. doi:10.4018/978-1-4666-6359-6.ch003

Aram, M., Koch, S., & Neumann, G. (2017). Long-Term Analysis of the Development of the Open ACS Community Framework. In F. Garcia-Peñalvo & A. García-Holgado (Eds.), *Open Source Solutions for Knowledge Management and Technological Ecosystems* (pp. 111–145). Hershey, PA: IGI Global. doi:10.4018/978-1-5225-0905-9.ch005

Armarego, J. (2014). Engaging Software Engineering Students with Employability Skills. In L. Yu (Ed.), *Overcoming Challenges in Software Engineering Education: Delivering Non-Technical Knowledge and Skills* (pp. 123–160). Hershey, PA: IGI Global. doi:10.4018/978-1-4666-5800-4.ch008

Bakar, A. D., Sultan, A. B., Zulzalil, H., & Din, J. (2014). Open Source Software Adaptation in Africa: Is a Matter of Inferior or Cheap is Not Quality? *International Journal of Open Source Software and Processes*, 5(1), 1–15. doi:10.4018/ijossp.2014010101

Barbosa, C., Alves, M. R., & Oliveira, B. (2016). Comparison of Methods to Display Principal Component Analysis, Focusing on Biplots and the Selection of Biplot Axes. In F. Miranda & C. Abreu (Eds.), *Handbook of Research on Computational Simulation and Modeling in Engineering* (pp. 289–332). Hershey, PA: IGI Global. doi:10.4018/978-1-4666-8823-0.ch010

Bermúdez, G. M., Arias, A. B., & Rojas, L. A. (2015). DSL TUNNOS Commerce: Model-Driven Architecture Applied to E-Commerce Platforms. In V. Díaz, J. Lovelle, & B. García-Bustelo (Eds.), *Handbook of Research on Innovations in Systems and Software Engineering* (pp. 500–509). Hershey, PA: IGI Global. doi:10.4018/978-1-4666-6359-6.ch020

Bibi, S., Katsaros, D., & Bozanis, P. (2015). Cloud Computing Economics. In V. Díaz, J. Lovelle, & B. García-Bustelo (Eds.), *Handbook of Research on Innovations in Systems and Software Engineering* (pp. 125–149). Hershey, PA: IGI Global. doi:10.4018/978-1-4666-6359-6.ch005

Bilotto, P. N., & Favre, L. (2016). Migrating JAVA to Mobile Platforms through HAXE: An MDD Approach. In A. Rosado da Cruz & S. Paiva (Eds.), *Modern Software Engineering Methodologies for Mobile and Cloud Environments* (pp. 240–268). Hershey, PA: IGI Global. doi:10.4018/978-1-4666-9916-8.ch013

Bishop, J. (2015). A Learning Organisation Approach to Software Project Management: Promoting Knowledge Transformation and Interprofessionalism through Crowd-Funded Agile Development. In A. Singh (Ed.), *Achieving Enterprise Agility through Innovative Software Development* (pp. 115–140). Hershey, PA: IGI Global. doi:10.4018/978-1-4666-8510-9.ch006

Bügler, M., & Borrmann, A. (2016). Simulation Based Construction Project Schedule Optimization: An Overview on the State-of-the-Art. In F. Miranda & C. Abreu (Eds.), *Handbook of Research on Computational Simulation and Modeling in Engineering* (pp. 482–507). Hershey, PA: IGI Global. doi:10.4018/978-1-4666-8823-0.ch016

Byers, D., & Shahmehri, N. (2015). Graphical Modeling of Security Goals and Software Vulnerabilities. In V. Díaz, J. Lovelle, & B. García-Bustelo (Eds.), *Handbook of Research on Innovations in Systems and Software Engineering* (pp. 1–31). Hershey, PA: IGI Global. doi:10.4018/978-1-4666-6359-6.ch001

Cassano, L., Cesarini, D., & Avvenuti, M. (2016). On the Use of Stochastic Activity Networks for an Energy-Aware Simulation of Automatic Weather Stations. In F. Miranda & C. Abreu (Eds.), *Handbook of Research on Computational Simulation and Modeling in Engineering* (pp. 184–207). Hershey, PA: IGI Global. doi:10.4018/978-1-4666-8823-0.ch006

Cawley, O., Weibelzahl, S., Richardson, I., & Delaney, Y. (2014). Incorporating a Self-Directed Learning Pedagogy in the Computing Classroom: Problem-Based Learning as a Means to Improving Software Engineering Learning Outcomes. In L. Yu (Ed.), *Overcoming Challenges in Software Engineering Education: Delivering Non-Technical Knowledge and Skills* (pp. 348–371). Hershey, PA: IGI Global. doi:10.4018/978-1-4666-5800-4.ch018

Chahal, K. K., & Saini, M. (2016). Open Source Software Evolution: A Systematic Literature Review (Part 1). *International Journal of Open Source Software and Processes, 7*(1), 1–27. doi:10.4018/IJOSSP.2016010101

Chahal, K. K., & Saini, M. (2016). Open Source Software Evolution: A Systematic Literature Review (Part 2). *International Journal of Open Source Software and Processes, 7*(1), 28–48. doi:10.4018/IJOSSP.2016010102

Chatzipoulidis, A., Michalopoulos, D., & Mavridis, I. (2016). Managing Enterprise IT Risks through Automated Security Metrics. In P. Papajorgji, F. Pinet, A. Guimarães, & J. Papathanasiou (Eds.), *Automated Enterprise Systems for Maximizing Business Performance* (pp. 215–243). Hershey, PA: IGI Global. doi:10.4018/978-1-4666-8841-4.ch012

Choudhary, A., & Baghel, A. S. (2016). Software Reliability Prediction Using Cuckoo Search Optimization, Empirical Mode Decomposition, and ARIMA Model: CS-EEMD-ARIMA Based SRGM. *International Journal of Open Source Software and Processes, 7*(4), 39–54. doi:10.4018/IJOSSP.2016100103

Clark, T., Barn, B., & Kulkarni, V. (2015). Modelling, Simulation, and Analysis for Enterprise Architecture. In V. Díaz, J. Lovelle, & B. García-Bustelo (Eds.), *Handbook of Research on Innovations in Systems and Software Engineering* (pp. 202–236). Hershey, PA: IGI Global. doi:10.4018/978-1-4666-6359-6.ch009

Constantinou, E., Ampatzoglou, A., & Stamelos, I. (2014). Quantifying Reuse in OSS: A Large-Scale Empirical Study. *International Journal of Open Source Software and Processes*, 5(3), 1–19. doi:10.4018/IJOSSP.2014070101

Corley, J., Syriani, E., Ergin, H., & Van Mierlo, S. (2016). Cloud-Based Multi-View Modeling Environments. In A. Rosado da Cruz & S. Paiva (Eds.), *Modern Software Engineering Methodologies for Mobile and Cloud Environments* (pp. 120–139). Hershey, PA: IGI Global. doi:10.4018/978-1-4666-9916-8.ch007

Costa, G., Lazouski, A., Martinelli, F., & Mori, P. (2015). Application Security for Mobile Devices. In V. Díaz, J. Lovelle, & B. García-Bustelo (Eds.), *Handbook of Research on Innovations in Systems and Software Engineering* (pp. 562–588). Hershey, PA: IGI Global. doi:10.4018/978-1-4666-6359-6.ch022

Damiani, L., Giribone, P., Guizzi, G., Revetria, R., & Romano, E. (2016). Different Approaches for Studying Interruptible Industrial Processes: Application of Two Different Simulation Techniques. In F. Miranda & C. Abreu (Eds.), *Handbook of Research on Computational Simulation and Modeling in Engineering* (pp. 69–104). Hershey, PA: IGI Global. doi:10.4018/978-1-4666-8823-0.ch002

Daoud, M. I., Alshalalfah, A., Awwad, F., & Al-Najar, M. (2014). A Freehand 3D Ultrasound Imaging System using Open-Source Software Tools with Improved Edge-Preserving Interpolation. *International Journal of Open Source Software and Processes*, 5(3), 39–57. doi:10.4018/IJOSSP.2014070103

David, B., & Chalon, R. (2015). Mobile Interaction in Real Augmented Environments: Principles, Platforms, Models, Formalisms, Development Processes, and Applications. In V. Díaz, J. Lovelle, & B. García-Bustelo (Eds.), *Handbook of Research on Innovations in Systems and Software Engineering* (pp. 511–561). Hershey, PA: IGI Global. doi:10.4018/978-1-4666-6359-6.ch021

Davis, J., & Chang, E. (2015). Optimized and Distributed Variant Logic for Model-Driven Applications. In V. Díaz, J. Lovelle, & B. García-Bustelo (Eds.), *Handbook of Research on Innovations in Systems and Software Engineering* (pp. 428–478). Hershey, PA: IGI Global. doi:10.4018/978-1-4666-6359-6. ch018

de Campos, A. Jr, Pozo, A. T., & Vergilio, S. R. (2016). Applying Evolutionary Many-Objective Optimization Algorithms to the Quality-Driven Web Service Composition Problem. In P. Papajorgji, F. Pinet, A. Guimarães, & J. Papathanasiou (Eds.), *Automated Enterprise Systems for Maximizing Business Performance* (pp. 170–194). Hershey, PA: IGI Global. doi:10.4018/978-1-4666-8841-4.ch010

Delgado, J. C. (2015). Decreasing Service Coupling to Increase Enterprise Agility. In A. Singh (Ed.), *Achieving Enterprise Agility through Innovative Software Development* (pp. 225–261). Hershey, PA: IGI Global. doi:10.4018/978-1-4666-8510-9.ch011

Delgado, J. M., Henriques, A. A., & Delgado, R. M. (2016). Structural Non-Linear Models and Simulation Techniques: An Efficient Combination for Safety Evaluation of RC Structures. In F. Miranda & C. Abreu (Eds.), *Handbook of Research on Computational Simulation and Modeling in Engineering* (pp. 540–584). Hershey, PA: IGI Global. doi:10.4018/978-1-4666-8823-0.ch018

Delgado, P. S., Arête, A., Pouca, N. V., & Costa, A. (2016). Numerical Modeling of RC Bridges for Seismic Risk Analysis. In F. Miranda & C. Abreu (Eds.), *Handbook of Research on Computational Simulation and Modeling in Engineering* (pp. 457–481). Hershey, PA: IGI Global. doi:10.4018/978-1-4666-8823-0.ch015

Deshpande, D. S., Kulkarni, P. R., & Metkewar, P. S. (2017). Need of the Research Community: Open Source Solution for Research Knowledge Management. In F. Garcia-Peñalvo & A. García-Holgado (Eds.), *Open Source Solutions for Knowledge Management and Technological Ecosystems* (pp. 146–174). Hershey, PA: IGI Global. doi:10.4018/978-1-5225-0905-9.ch006

Díaz-Moreno, P., Carrasco, J. J., Soria-Olivas, E., Martínez-Martínez, J. M., Escandell-Montero, P., & Gómez-Sanchis, J. (2016). Educational Software Based on Matlab GUIs for Neural Networks Courses. In F. Miranda & C. Abreu (Eds.), *Handbook of Research on Computational Simulation and Modeling in Engineering* (pp. 333–358). Hershey, PA: IGI Global. doi:10.4018/978-1-4666-8823-0.ch011

Dragan, D., Petrovic, V. B., & Ivetic, D. (2016). Methods for Assessing Still Image Compression Efficiency: PACS Example. In F. Miranda & C. Abreu (Eds.), *Handbook of Research on Computational Simulation and Modeling in Engineering* (pp. 389–416). Hershey, PA: IGI Global. doi:10.4018/978-1-4666-8823-0.ch013

Dubielewicz, I., Hnatkowska, B., Huzar, Z., & Tuzinkiewicz, L. (2015). Quality-Driven Database System Development within MDA Approach. In V. Díaz, J. Lovelle, & B. García-Bustelo (Eds.), *Handbook of Research on Innovations in Systems and Software Engineering* (pp. 237–268). Hershey, PA: IGI Global. doi:10.4018/978-1-4666-6359-6.ch010

Duran, R. E., & Duc Do, A. (2015). Multichannel Service Delivery Architecture: A Case Study. In V. Díaz, J. Lovelle, & B. García-Bustelo (Eds.), *Handbook of Research on Innovations in Systems and Software Engineering* (pp. 589–601). Hershey, PA: IGI Global. doi:10.4018/978-1-4666-6359-6.ch023

Farooq, S. U., & Quadri, S. M. (2016). Test Cloud before Cloud Test. In A. Rosado da Cruz & S. Paiva (Eds.), *Modern Software Engineering Methodologies for Mobile and Cloud Environments* (pp. 89–101). Hershey, PA: IGI Global. doi:10.4018/978-1-4666-9916-8.ch005

Favre, L., Martinez, L., & Pereira, C. (2015). Reverse Engineering of Object-Oriented Code: An ADM Approach. In V. Díaz, J. Lovelle, & B. García-Bustelo (Eds.), *Handbook of Research on Innovations in Systems and Software Engineering* (pp. 386–410). Hershey, PA: IGI Global. doi:10.4018/978-1-4666-6359-6.ch016

Fernandes, J. M., & Ferreira, A. L. (2016). Quality Attributes for Mobile Applications. In A. Rosado da Cruz & S. Paiva (Eds.), *Modern Software Engineering Methodologies for Mobile and Cloud Environments* (pp. 141–154). Hershey, PA: IGI Global. doi:10.4018/978-1-4666-9916-8.ch008

Galanis, N., Mayol, E., Casany, M. J., & Alier, M. (2017). Tools Interoperability for Learning Management Systems. In F. Garcia-Peñalvo & A. García-Holgado (Eds.), *Open Source Solutions for Knowledge Management and Technological Ecosystems* (pp. 25–49). Hershey, PA: IGI Global. doi:10.4018/978-1-5225-0905-9.ch002

García, C. G., & Espada, J. P. (2015). MUSPEL: Generation of Applications to Interconnect Heterogeneous Objects Using Model-Driven Engineering. In V. Díaz, J. Lovelle, & B. García-Bustelo (Eds.), *Handbook of Research on Innovations in Systems and Software Engineering* (pp. 365–385). Hershey, PA: IGI Global. doi:10.4018/978-1-4666-6359-6.ch015

García-Peñalvo, F. J., Hernández-García, Á., Conde, M. Á., Fidalgo-Blanco, Á., Sein-Echaluce, M. L., Alier-Forment, M., & Iglesias-Pradas, S. et al. (2017). Enhancing Education for the Knowledge Society Era with Learning Ecosystems. In F. Garcia-Peñalvo & A. García-Holgado (Eds.), *Open Source Solutions for Knowledge Management and Technological Ecosystems* (pp. 1–24). Hershey, PA: IGI Global. doi:10.4018/978-1-5225-0905-9.ch001

Gaspar, P. D., Dinho da Silva, P., Gonçalves, J. P., & Carneiro, R. (2016). Computational Modelling and Simulation to Assist the Improvement of Thermal Performance and Energy Efficiency in Industrial Engineering Systems: Application to Cold Stores. In F. Miranda & C. Abreu (Eds.), *Handbook of Research on Computational Simulation and Modeling in Engineering* (pp. 1–68). Hershey, PA: IGI Global. doi:10.4018/978-1-4666-8823-0.ch001

Gates, A. Q., Villa, E. Y., & Salamah, S. (2014). Developing Communities of Practice to Prepare Software Engineers with Effective Team Skills. In L. Yu (Ed.), *Overcoming Challenges in Software Engineering Education: Delivering Non-Technical Knowledge and Skills* (pp. 52–70). Hershey, PA: IGI Global. doi:10.4018/978-1-4666-5800-4.ch004

Gerlach, J. H., Wu, C., Cunningham, L. F., & Young, C. E. (2016). An Exploratory Study of Conflict over Paying Debian Developers. *International Journal of Open Source Software and Processes*, 7(3), 20–38. doi:10.4018/IJOSSP.2016070102

Ghafele, R., & Gibert, B. (2014). Open Growth: The Impact of Open Source Software on Employment in the USA. *International Journal of Open Source Software and Processes*, 5(1), 16–49. doi:10.4018/ijossp.2014010102

Gharzouli, M. (2016). Reuse and Improvement of Peersim Open Source Packages: A Case Study with Chord and Cloudcast. *International Journal of Open Source Software and Processes*, 7(3), 39–55. doi:10.4018/IJOSSP.2016070103

Gianni, M., & Gotzamani, K. (2016). Integrated Management Systems and Information Management Systems: Common Threads. In P. Papajorgji, F. Pinet, A. Guimarães, & J. Papathanasiou (Eds.), *Automated Enterprise Systems for Maximizing Business Performance* (pp. 195–214). Hershey, PA: IGI Global. doi:10.4018/978-1-4666-8841-4.ch011

Goel, N. (2015). Legacy Systems towards Aspect-Oriented Systems. In A. Singh (Ed.), *Achieving Enterprise Agility through Innovative Software Development* (pp. 262–286). Hershey, PA: IGI Global. doi:10.4018/978-1-4666-8510-9.ch012

Goyal, A., & Sardana, N. (2016). Analytical Study on Bug Triaging Practices. *International Journal of Open Source Software and Processes*, 7(2), 20–42. doi:10.4018/IJOSSP.2016040102

Guendouz, M., Amine, A., & Hamou, R. M. (2015). Recommending Relevant Open Source Projects on GitHub using a Collaborative-Filtering Technique. *International Journal of Open Source Software and Processes*, 6(1), 1–16. doi:10.4018/IJOSSP.2015010101

Guetmi, N., & Imine, A. (2016). Designing Mobile Collaborative Applications for Cloud Environments. In A. Rosado da Cruz & S. Paiva (Eds.), *Modern Software Engineering Methodologies for Mobile and Cloud Environments* (pp. 34–60). Hershey, PA: IGI Global. doi:10.4018/978-1-4666-9916-8.ch003

Hanandeh, F., Al-Shannag, M. Y., & Alkhaffaf, M. M. (2016). Using Data Mining Techniques with Open Source Software to Evaluate the Various Factors Affecting Academic Performance: A Case Study of Students in the Faculty of Information Technology. *International Journal of Open Source Software and Processes*, 7(2), 72–92. doi:10.4018/IJOSSP.2016040104

Harmanen, J., & Mikkonen, T. (2016). On Polyglot Programming in the Web. In A. Rosado da Cruz & S. Paiva (Eds.), *Modern Software Engineering Methodologies for Mobile and Cloud Environments* (pp. 102–119). Hershey, PA: IGI Global. doi:10.4018/978-1-4666-9916-8.ch006

Hein, D., & Saiedian, H. (2015). Reasoning Qualitatively about Handheld Multimedia Framework Quality Attributes. In V. Díaz, J. Lovelle, & B. García-Bustelo (Eds.), *Handbook of Research on Innovations in Systems and Software Engineering* (pp. 731–745). Hershey, PA: IGI Global. doi:10.4018/978-1-4666-6359-6.ch028

Heni, N., & Hamam, H. (2016). Databases and Information Systems. In P. Papajorgji, F. Pinet, A. Guimarães, & J. Papathanasiou (Eds.), *Automated Enterprise Systems for Maximizing Business Performance* (pp. 123–149). Hershey, PA: IGI Global. doi:10.4018/978-1-4666-8841-4.ch008

Hermanns, T., Thombansen, U., Nießen, M., Jansen, U., & Schulz, W. (2016). Modeling for Self-Optimization in Laser Cutting. In F. Miranda & C. Abreu (Eds.), *Handbook of Research on Computational Simulation and Modeling in Engineering* (pp. 586–617). Hershey, PA: IGI Global. doi:10.4018/978-1-4666-8823-0.ch019

Hernández, G. I., Fuente, A. A., Pérez, B. L., & Núñez-Valdéz, E. R. (2015). Rule-Based Domain-Specific Modeling for E-Government Service Transactions. In V. Díaz, J. Lovelle, & B. García-Bustelo (Eds.), *Handbook of Research on Innovations in Systems and Software Engineering* (pp. 269–282). Hershey, PA: IGI Global. doi:10.4018/978-1-4666-6359-6.ch011

Hoffert, J., Schmidt, D. C., & Gokhale, A. (2015). Quantitative Productivity Analysis of a Domain-Specific Modeling Language. In V. Díaz, J. Lovelle, & B. García-Bustelo (Eds.), *Handbook of Research on Innovations in Systems and Software Engineering* (pp. 313–344). Hershey, PA: IGI Global. doi:10.4018/978-1-4666-6359-6.ch013

Huang, J. S., Kozaki, K., & Kumazawa, T. (2017). Knowledge Structuring for Sustainable Development and the Hozo Tool. In F. Garcia-Peñalvo & A. García-Holgado (Eds.), *Open Source Solutions for Knowledge Management and Technological Ecosystems* (pp. 195–221). Hershey, PA: IGI Global. doi:10.4018/978-1-5225-0905-9.ch008

Ilayperuma, T., & Zdravkovic, J. (2015). Using Business Value Models to Elicit Services Conducting Business Transactions. In V. Díaz, J. Lovelle, & B. García-Bustelo (Eds.), *Handbook of Research on Innovations in Systems and Software Engineering* (pp. 98–124). Hershey, PA: IGI Global. doi:10.4018/978-1-4666-6359-6.ch004

Imre, Ö. (2017). Trying to Go Open: Knowledge Management in an Academic Journal. In F. Garcia-Peñalvo & A. García-Holgado (Eds.), *Open Source Solutions for Knowledge Management and Technological Ecosystems* (pp. 222–250). Hershey, PA: IGI Global. doi:10.4018/978-1-5225-0905-9.ch009

Inayat, I., Salim, S. S., & Marczak, S. (2015). Communication and Awareness Patterns of Distributed Agile Teams. In A. Singh (Ed.), *Achieving Enterprise Agility through Innovative Software Development* (pp. 1–16). Hershey, PA: IGI Global. doi:10.4018/978-1-4666-8510-9.ch001

Ivanović, M., Budimac, Z., Putnik, Z., & Komlenov, Ž. (2014). Encouraging Teamwork, Web 2.0, and Social Networking Elements in Distance Learning. In L. Yu (Ed.), *Overcoming Challenges in Software Engineering Education: Delivering Non-Technical Knowledge and Skills* (pp. 71–90). Hershey, PA: IGI Global. doi:10.4018/978-1-4666-5800-4.ch005

Jain, A., Tayal, D. K., Khari, M., & Vij, S. (2016). A Novel Method for Test Path Prioritization using Centrality Measures. *International Journal of Open Source Software and Processes*, 7(4), 19–38. doi:10.4018/IJOSSP.2016100102

Johns-Boast, L. (2014). Developing Personal and Professional Skills in Software Engineering Students. In L. Yu (Ed.), *Overcoming Challenges in Software Engineering Education: Delivering Non-Technical Knowledge and Skills* (pp. 198–228). Hershey, PA: IGI Global. doi:10.4018/978-1-4666-5800-4.ch011

Kaliyeva, K. (2016). Energy Conservation Law for the Turbulent Motion in the Free Atmosphere: Turbulent Motion in the Free Atmosphere. In F. Miranda & C. Abreu (Eds.), *Handbook of Research on Computational Simulation and Modeling in Engineering* (pp. 105–138). Hershey, PA: IGI Global. doi:10.4018/978-1-4666-8823-0.ch003

Kalnins, A., Straszak, T., Śmiałek, M., Kalnina, E., Celms, E., & Nowakowski, W. (2015). Developing Software with Domain-Driven Model Reuse. In V. Díaz, J. Lovelle, & B. García-Bustelo (Eds.), *Handbook of Research on Innovations in Systems and Software Engineering* (pp. 283–312). Hershey, PA: IGI Global. doi:10.4018/978-1-4666-6359-6.ch012

Kamthan, P. (2014). Towards an Understanding of Collaborations in Agile Course Projects. In L. Yu (Ed.), *Overcoming Challenges in Software Engineering Education: Delivering Non-Technical Knowledge and Skills* (pp. 36–51). Hershey, PA: IGI Global. doi:10.4018/978-1-4666-5800-4.ch003

Kang, M., Pinet, F., Bimonte, S., De Sousa, G., & Chanet, J. (2016). Use of Sensor Data Warehouse for Soil Moisture Analysis. In P. Papajorgji, F. Pinet, A. Guimarães, & J. Papathanasiou (Eds.), *Automated Enterprise Systems for Maximizing Business Performance* (pp. 43–57). Hershey, PA: IGI Global. doi:10.4018/978-1-4666-8841-4.ch003

Kasemsap, K. (2015). The Role of Business Process Reengineering in the Modern Business World. In A. Singh (Ed.), *Achieving Enterprise Agility through Innovative Software Development* (pp. 87–114). Hershey, PA: IGI Global. doi:10.4018/978-1-4666-8510-9.ch005

Kaur, D. (2015). Lean Manufacturing to Lean IT: An Emerging Quality Assurance Methodology in IT. In A. Singh (Ed.), *Achieving Enterprise Agility through Innovative Software Development* (pp. 67–86). Hershey, PA: IGI Global. doi:10.4018/978-1-4666-8510-9.ch004

Khanh, D. V., Vasant, P. M., Elamvazuthi, I., & Dieu, V. N. (2016). Multi-Objective Optimization of Two-Stage Thermo-Electric Cooler Using Differential Evolution: MO Optimization of TEC Using DE. In F. Miranda & C. Abreu (Eds.), *Handbook of Research on Computational Simulation and Modeling in Engineering* (pp. 139–170). Hershey, PA: IGI Global. doi:10.4018/978-1-4666-8823-0.ch004

Kose, U. (2014). On the State of Free and Open Source E-Learning 2.0 Software. *International Journal of Open Source Software and Processes, 5*(2), 55–75. doi:10.4018/ijossp.2014040103

Kuhrmann, M., Femmer, H., & Eckhardt, J. (2014). Controlled Experiments as Means to Teach Soft Skills in Software Engineering. In L. Yu (Ed.), *Overcoming Challenges in Software Engineering Education: Delivering Non-Technical Knowledge and Skills* (pp. 180–197). Hershey, PA: IGI Global. doi:10.4018/978-1-4666-5800-4.ch010

Kukreja, V., & Singh, A. (2015). Agile Enablers and Adoption Scenario in Industry Context. In A. Singh (Ed.), *Achieving Enterprise Agility through Innovative Software Development* (pp. 157–178). Hershey, PA: IGI Global. doi:10.4018/978-1-4666-8510-9.ch008

Kumar, S., & Raj, B. (2016). Simulations and Modeling of TFET for Low Power Design. In F. Miranda & C. Abreu (Eds.), *Handbook of Research on Computational Simulation and Modeling in Engineering* (pp. 640–667). Hershey, PA: IGI Global. doi:10.4018/978-1-4666-8823-0.ch021

Lacy, F. (2016). Using Theoretical and Computational Models to Understand How Metals Function as Temperature Sensors. In F. Miranda & C. Abreu (Eds.), *Handbook of Research on Computational Simulation and Modeling in Engineering* (pp. 668–702). Hershey, PA: IGI Global. doi:10.4018/978-1-4666-8823-0.ch022

Lahmiri, S. (2016). On Simulation Performance of Feedforward and NARX Networks Under Different Numerical Training Algorithms. In F. Miranda & C. Abreu (Eds.), *Handbook of Research on Computational Simulation and Modeling in Engineering* (pp. 171–183). Hershey, PA: IGI Global. doi:10.4018/978-1-4666-8823-0.ch005

Lainez, M., Deville, Y., Dessy, A., Dejemeppe, C., Mairy, J., & Van Cauwelaert, S. (2014). A Project-Based Introduction to Agile Software Development. In L. Yu (Ed.), *Overcoming Challenges in Software Engineering Education: Delivering Non-Technical Knowledge and Skills* (pp. 277–294). Hershey, PA: IGI Global. doi:10.4018/978-1-4666-5800-4.ch014

Lal, S., Sardana, N., & Sureka, A. (2015). Two Level Empirical Study of Logging Statements in Open Source Java Projects. *International Journal of Open Source Software and Processes*, 6(1), 49–73. doi:10.4018/IJOSSP.2015010104

Lal, S., Sardana, N., & Sureka, A. (2016). Improving Logging Prediction on Imbalanced Datasets: A Case Study on Open Source Java Projects. *International Journal of Open Source Software and Processes*, 7(2), 43–71. doi:10.4018/IJOSSP.2016040103

Laminu, M., AbdulAzeez, B., & Yousef, S. (2016). SIP-PMIP Cross-Layer Mobility Management Scheme. In A. Rosado da Cruz, & S. Paiva (Eds.), *Modern Software Engineering Methodologies for Mobile and Cloud Environments* (pp. 285-321). Hershey, PA: IGI Global. doi:10.4018/978-1-4666-9916-8.ch015

Lano, K., & Kolahdouz-Rahimi, S. (2015). High-Integrity Model-Based Development. In V. Díaz, J. Lovelle, & B. García-Bustelo (Eds.), *Handbook of Research on Innovations in Systems and Software Engineering* (pp. 479–499). Hershey, PA: IGI Global. doi:10.4018/978-1-4666-6359-6.ch019

Le Goaer, O., Barbier, F., & Cariou, E. (2016). Android Executable Modeling: Beyond Android Programming. In A. Rosado da Cruz & S. Paiva (Eds.), *Modern Software Engineering Methodologies for Mobile and Cloud Environments* (pp. 269–283). Hershey, PA: IGI Global. doi:10.4018/978-1-4666-9916-8.ch014

MacKellar, B. K., Sabin, M., & Tucker, A. B. (2014). Bridging the Academia-Industry Gap in Software Engineering: A Client-Oriented Open Source Software Projects Course. In L. Yu (Ed.), *Overcoming Challenges in Software Engineering Education: Delivering Non-Technical Knowledge and Skills* (pp. 373–396). Hershey, PA: IGI Global. doi:10.4018/978-1-4666-5800-4.ch019

Madan, K. (2015). Motivation behind Agile Software Development over Traditional Development. In A. Singh (Ed.), *Achieving Enterprise Agility through Innovative Software Development* (pp. 141–156). Hershey, PA: IGI Global. doi:10.4018/978-1-4666-8510-9.ch007

Mala, D. J. (2016). A Study on Software Development Architectures for Mobile Cloud Computing (MCC) for Green IT: A Conceptual Mobile Cloud Architecture Using Artificial Bee Colony-Based Approach. In A. Rosado da Cruz & S. Paiva (Eds.), *Modern Software Engineering Methodologies for Mobile and Cloud Environments* (pp. 21–33). Hershey, PA: IGI Global. doi:10.4018/978-1-4666-9916-8.ch002

Manthou, V., Bialas, C., & Stefanou, C. J. (2016). Benefits and Barriers of E-Sourcing and E-Purchasing in the Healthcare Sector: A Case Study. In P. Papajorgji, F. Pinet, A. Guimarães, & J. Papathanasiou (Eds.), *Automated Enterprise Systems for Maximizing Business Performance* (pp. 71–87). Hershey, PA: IGI Global. doi:10.4018/978-1-4666-8841-4.ch005

Manthou, V., Stefanou, C. J., & Tigka, K. (2016). The Evaluation of Business Performance in ERP Environments. In P. Papajorgji, F. Pinet, A. Guimarães, & J. Papathanasiou (Eds.), *Automated Enterprise Systems for Maximizing Business Performance* (pp. 88–96). Hershey, PA: IGI Global. doi:10.4018/978-1-4666-8841-4.ch006

Markkula, J., & Mazhelis, O. (2015). A Generic Architectural Model Approach for Efficient Utilization of Patterns: Application in the Mobile Domain. In V. Díaz, J. Lovelle, & B. García-Bustelo (Eds.), *Handbook of Research on Innovations in Systems and Software Engineering* (pp. 682–709). Hershey, PA: IGI Global. doi:10.4018/978-1-4666-6359-6.ch026

Martínez, E. M., Mesa, J. M., Bollati, V. A., & López-Sanz, M. (2014). Applying Coaching Practices to Leadership and Team Management Learning in Computer Science: A Practical Experience. In L. Yu (Ed.), *Overcoming Challenges in Software Engineering Education: Delivering Non-Technical Knowledge and Skills* (pp. 18–34). Hershey, PA: IGI Global. doi:10.4018/978-1-4666-5800-4.ch002

Misra, R., Panigrahi, C. R., Panda, B., & Pati, B. (2016). Software Design. In F. Miranda & C. Abreu (Eds.), *Handbook of Research on Computational Simulation and Modeling in Engineering* (pp. 417–455). Hershey, PA: IGI Global. doi:10.4018/978-1-4666-8823-0.ch014

Misra, S., & Adewumi, A. (2015). Object-Oriented Cognitive Complexity Measures: An Analysis. In V. Díaz, J. Lovelle, & B. García-Bustelo (Eds.), *Handbook of Research on Innovations in Systems and Software Engineering* (pp. 150–170). Hershey, PA: IGI Global. doi:10.4018/978-1-4666-6359-6.ch006

Misra, S., Omorodion, M., Mishra, A., & Fernandez, L. (2015). A Proposed Pragmatic Software Development Process Model. In V. Díaz, J. Lovelle, & B. García-Bustelo (Eds.), *Handbook of Research on Innovations in Systems and Software Engineering* (pp. 186–200). Hershey, PA: IGI Global. doi:10.4018/978-1-4666-6359-6.ch008

Molina-Carmona, R., Compañ-Rosique, P., Satorre-Cuerda, R., Villagrá-Arnedo, C. J., Gallego-Durán, F. J., & Llorens-Largo, F. (2017). Technological Ecosystem Maps for IT Governance: Application to a Higher Education Institution. In F. Garcia-Peñalvo & A. García-Holgado (Eds.), *Open Source Solutions for Knowledge Management and Technological Ecosystems* (pp. 50–80). Hershey, PA: IGI Global. doi:10.4018/978-1-5225-0905-9.ch003

Monsalve, E. S., Pereira, A. X., & Werneck, V. M. (2014). Teaching Software Engineering through a Collaborative Game. In L. Yu (Ed.), *Overcoming Challenges in Software Engineering Education: Delivering Non-Technical Knowledge and Skills* (pp. 310–331). Hershey, PA: IGI Global. doi:10.4018/978-1-4666-5800-4.ch016

Motogna, S., Lazăr, I., & Pârv, B. (2015). Developing Executable UML Components Based on fUML and Alf. In V. Díaz, J. Lovelle, & B. García-Bustelo (Eds.), *Handbook of Research on Innovations in Systems and Software Engineering* (pp. 345–364). Hershey, PA: IGI Global. doi:10.4018/978-1-4666-6359-6.ch014

Mushiri, T., & Mbohwa, C. (2016). Simulation and Modeling: Design of a Fuzzy Logic Based Hydraulic Turbine Governing System. In F. Miranda & C. Abreu (Eds.), *Handbook of Research on Computational Simulation and Modeling in Engineering* (pp. 225–259). Hershey, PA: IGI Global. doi:10.4018/978-1-4666-8823-0.ch008

Ncibi, F., Hamam, H., & Ben Braiek, E. (2016). Android for Enterprise Automated Systems. In P. Papajorgji, F. Pinet, A. Guimarães, & J. Papathanasiou (Eds.), *Automated Enterprise Systems for Maximizing Business Performance* (pp. 19–42). Hershey, PA: IGI Global. doi:10.4018/978-1-4666-8841-4.ch002

Ndjodo, M. F., & Ngah, V. B. (2014). From Textual Analysis to Requirements Elicitation. In L. Yu (Ed.), *Overcoming Challenges in Software Engineering Education: Delivering Non-Technical Knowledge and Skills* (pp. 92–110). Hershey, PA: IGI Global. doi:10.4018/978-1-4666-5800-4.ch006

Nishani, L. (2016). Review on Security Threats for Mobile Devices and Significant Countermeasures on Securing Android Mobiles. In P. Papajorgji, F. Pinet, A. Guimarães, & J. Papathanasiou (Eds.), *Automated Enterprise Systems for Maximizing Business Performance* (pp. 1–18). Hershey, PA: IGI Global. doi:10.4018/978-1-4666-8841-4.ch001

Nunes, J. F., Moreira, P. M., & Tavares, J. M. (2016). Human Motion Analysis and Simulation Tools: A Survey. In F. Miranda & C. Abreu (Eds.), *Handbook of Research on Computational Simulation and Modeling in Engineering* (pp. 359–388). Hershey, PA: IGI Global. doi:10.4018/978-1-4666-8823-0.ch012

Ortmann, S., & Langendoerfer, P. (2015). Autonomous Execution of Reliable Sensor Network Applications on Varying Node Hardware. In V. Díaz, J. Lovelle, & B. García-Bustelo (Eds.), *Handbook of Research on Innovations in Systems and Software Engineering* (pp. 602–663). Hershey, PA: IGI Global. doi:10.4018/978-1-4666-6359-6.ch024

Osis, J., & Asnina, E. (2015). Is Modeling a Treatment for the Weakness of Software Engineering? In V. Díaz, J. Lovelle, & B. García-Bustelo (Eds.), *Handbook of Research on Innovations in Systems and Software Engineering* (pp. 411–427). Hershey, PA: IGI Global. doi:10.4018/978-1-4666-6359-6.ch017

Page, T. (2015). Should Open-Source Technology be used in Design Education? *International Journal of Open Source Software and Processes*, 6(1), 17–30. doi:10.4018/IJOSSP.2015010102

Pang, C. (2015). A Cross-Platform Architecture with Intelligent Agents for Dynamic Processes and Services Composition. In A. Singh (Ed.), *Achieving Enterprise Agility through Innovative Software Development* (pp. 36–66). Hershey, PA: IGI Global. doi:10.4018/978-1-4666-8510-9.ch003

Pereira da Silva, J. A., Paiva, S., & Rosado da Cruz, A. M. (2016). Model-Driven Development of Data-Centered Mobile Applications: A Case Study for Android. In A. Rosado da Cruz & S. Paiva (Eds.), *Modern Software Engineering Methodologies for Mobile and Cloud Environments* (pp. 213–239). Hershey, PA: IGI Global. doi:10.4018/978-1-4666-9916-8.ch012

Periyasamy, K. (2014). Teaching Software Project Management. In L. Yu (Ed.), *Overcoming Challenges in Software Engineering Education: Delivering Non-Technical Knowledge and Skills* (pp. 1–17). Hershey, PA: IGI Global. doi:10.4018/978-1-4666-5800-4.ch001

Pina, P. (2017). Free and Open Source Software Movements as Agents of an Alternative Use of Copyright Law. In S. Gordon (Ed.), *Online Communities as Agents of Change and Social Movements* (pp. 253–270). Hershey, PA: IGI Global. doi:10.4018/978-1-5225-2495-3.ch010

Pinet, F., Carluer, N., Lauvernet, C., Cheviron, B., Bimonte, S., & Miralles, A. (2016). Storage of Simulation Result Data: A Database Perspective. In P. Papajorgji, F. Pinet, A. Guimarães, & J. Papathanasiou (Eds.), *Automated Enterprise Systems for Maximizing Business Performance* (pp. 58–70). Hershey, PA: IGI Global. doi:10.4018/978-1-4666-8841-4.ch004

Pinto, P., Pinto, A. A., & Ricardo, M. (2016). Reducing Simulation Runtime in Wireless Sensor Networks: A Simulation Framework to Reduce WSN Simulation Runtime by Using Multiple Simultaneous Instances. In F. Miranda & C. Abreu (Eds.), *Handbook of Research on Computational Simulation and Modeling in Engineering* (pp. 726–741). Hershey, PA: IGI Global. doi:10.4018/978-1-4666-8823-0.ch024

Quintão, J. P., Pereira, L., & Paiva, S. (2016). A Domain Independent Pedestrian Dead Reckoning System Solution for Android Smartphones. In A. Rosado da Cruz & S. Paiva (Eds.), *Modern Software Engineering Methodologies for Mobile and Cloud Environments* (pp. 195–211). Hershey, PA: IGI Global. doi:10.4018/978-1-4666-9916-8.ch011

Rajapakse, D. C. (2014). Peer Feedback in Software Engineering Courses. In L. Yu (Ed.), *Overcoming Challenges in Software Engineering Education: Delivering Non-Technical Knowledge and Skills* (pp. 111–121). Hershey, PA: IGI Global. doi:10.4018/978-1-4666-5800-4.ch007

Ramingwong, S., & Ramingwong, L. (2014). ECSE: A Pseudo-SDLC Game for Software Engineering Class. In L. Yu (Ed.), *Overcoming Challenges in Software Engineering Education: Delivering Non-Technical Knowledge and Skills* (pp. 296–309). Hershey, PA: IGI Global. doi:10.4018/978-1-4666-5800-4.ch015

Ratti, N., & Kaur, P. (2015). Applicability of Lehman Laws on Open Source Evolution. In A. Singh (Ed.), *Achieving Enterprise Agility through Innovative Software Development* (pp. 199–224). Hershey, PA: IGI Global. doi:10.4018/978-1-4666-8510-9.ch010

Rjaibi, N., Rabai, L. B., & Mili, A. (2015). The MFC Cybersecurity Model Extension and Diagnostic toward a Depth Measurement: E-Learning Systems Case Study. In A. Singh (Ed.), *Achieving Enterprise Agility through Innovative Software Development* (pp. 179–198). Hershey, PA: IGI Global. doi:10.4018/978-1-4666-8510-9.ch009

Rodríguez, A. V., Mateos, C., Zunino, A., & Longo, M. (2016). An Analysis of the Effects of Bad Smell-Driven Refactorings in Mobile Applications on Battery Usage. In A. Rosado da Cruz & S. Paiva (Eds.), *Modern Software Engineering Methodologies for Mobile and Cloud Environments* (pp. 155–175). Hershey, PA: IGI Global. doi:10.4018/978-1-4666-9916-8.ch009

Rosado da Cruz, A. M., & Paiva, S. (2016). Cloud and Mobile: A Future Together. In A. Rosado da Cruz & S. Paiva (Eds.), *Modern Software Engineering Methodologies for Mobile and Cloud Environments* (pp. 1–20). Hershey, PA: IGI Global. doi:10.4018/978-1-4666-9916-8.ch001

Roussaki, I., Kalatzis, N., Liampotis, N., Kosmides, P., Anagnostou, M., & Sykas, E. (2015). Putting Personal Smart Spaces into Context. In V. Díaz, J. Lovelle, & B. García-Bustelo (Eds.), *Handbook of Research on Innovations in Systems and Software Engineering* (pp. 710–730). Hershey, PA: IGI Global. doi:10.4018/978-1-4666-6359-6.ch027

Saeeda, H., Arif, F., & Minhas, N. M. (2016). Usability Software Engineering Testing Experimentation for Android-Based Web Applications: Usability Engineering Testing for Online Learning Management System. In A. Rosado da Cruz & S. Paiva (Eds.), *Modern Software Engineering Methodologies for Mobile and Cloud Environments* (pp. 176–194). Hershey, PA: IGI Global. doi:10.4018/978-1-4666-9916-8.ch010

Salamah, S., Towhidnejad, M., & Hilburn, T. (2014). Digital Home: A Case Study Approach to Teaching Software Engineering Concepts. In L. Yu (Ed.), *Overcoming Challenges in Software Engineering Education: Delivering Non-Technical Knowledge and Skills* (pp. 333–347). Hershey, PA: IGI Global. doi:10.4018/978-1-4666-5800-4.ch017

Sawicki, S., Frantz, R. Z., Fernandes, V. M., Roos-Frantz, F., Yevseyeva, I., & Corchuelo, R. (2016). Characterising Enterprise Application Integration Solutions as Discrete-Event Systems. In F. Miranda & C. Abreu (Eds.), *Handbook of Research on Computational Simulation and Modeling in Engineering* (pp. 261–288). Hershey, PA: IGI Global. doi:10.4018/978-1-4666-8823-0.ch009

Schmidt, H., Hatebur, D., & Heisel, M. (2015). Developing Secure Software Using UML Patterns. In V. Díaz, J. Lovelle, & B. García-Bustelo (Eds.), *Handbook of Research on Innovations in Systems and Software Engineering* (pp. 32–70). Hershey, PA: IGI Global. doi:10.4018/978-1-4666-6359-6.ch002

Schuster, D. W. (2017). Selection Process for Free Open Source Software. In E. Iglesias (Ed.), *Library Technology Funding, Planning, and Deployment* (pp. 55–71). Hershey, PA: IGI Global. doi:10.4018/978-1-5225-1735-1.ch004

Scott, E., Rodríguez, G., Soria, Á., & Campo, M. (2014). Experiences in Software Engineering Education: Using Scrum, Agile Coaching, and Virtual Reality. In L. Yu (Ed.), *Overcoming Challenges in Software Engineering Education: Delivering Non-Technical Knowledge and Skills* (pp. 250–276). Hershey, PA: IGI Global. doi:10.4018/978-1-4666-5800-4.ch013

Sedelmaier, Y., & Landes, D. (2014). Practicing Soft Skills in Software Engineering: A Project-Based Didactical Approach. In L. Yu (Ed.), *Overcoming Challenges in Software Engineering Education: Delivering Non-Technical Knowledge and Skills* (pp. 161–179). Hershey, PA: IGI Global. doi:10.4018/978-1-4666-5800-4.ch009

Seppänen, M., & Helander, N. (2014). Creating Value through Business Models in Open Source Software. *International Journal of Open Source Software and Processes*, 5(2), 40–54. doi:10.4018/ijossp.2014040102

Showole, A. A. (2015). Open Source Developer Layer Assessment: Open Onion. *International Journal of Open Source Software and Processes*, 6(1), 31–48. doi:10.4018/IJOSSP.2015010103

Singh, B., & Panda, S. N. (2015). A Proactive Approach to Intrusion Detection in Cloud Software as a Service. In A. Singh (Ed.), *Achieving Enterprise Agility through Innovative Software Development* (pp. 287–305). Hershey, PA: IGI Global. doi:10.4018/978-1-4666-8510-9.ch013

Srihi, S., Fnaiech, F., Balti, A., & Hamam, H. (2016). Information Security: Application in Business to Maximize the Security and Protect Confidential and Private Data. In P. Papajorgji, F. Pinet, A. Guimarães, & J. Papathanasiou (Eds.), *Automated Enterprise Systems for Maximizing Business Performance* (pp. 244–266). Hershey, PA: IGI Global. doi:10.4018/978-1-4666-8841-4.ch013

Štavljanin, V., & Minović, M. (2017). Gamification Ecosystems: Current State and Perspectives. In F. Garcia-Peñalvo & A. García-Holgado (Eds.), *Open Source Solutions for Knowledge Management and Technological Ecosystems* (pp. 81–110). Hershey, PA: IGI Global. doi:10.4018/978-1-5225-0905-9.ch004

Subburaman, D., Jagan, J., Dalkiliç, Y., & Samui, P. (2016). Reliability Analysis of Slope Using MPMR, GRNN and GPR. In F. Miranda & C. Abreu (Eds.), *Handbook of Research on Computational Simulation and Modeling in Engineering* (pp. 208–224). Hershey, PA: IGI Global. doi:10.4018/978-1-4666-8823-0.ch007

Swanson, P. (2014). Novice Language Teachers Selection Criteria and Uses for Digital Voice Recording Software. *International Journal of Open Source Software and Processes*, 5(1), 66–79. doi:10.4018/ijossp.2014010104

Syeed, M. M., Hammouda, I., & Systä, T. (2014). Prediction Models and Techniques for Open Source Software Projects: A Systematic Literature Review. *International Journal of Open Source Software and Processes*, 5(2), 1–39. doi:10.4018/ijossp.2014040101

Tolu, H. (2014). Position Paper: Misconceptions & Discriminations in the Software Decision Making Process in Turkey. *International Journal of Open Source Software and Processes*, 5(3), 20–38. doi:10.4018/IJOSSP.2014070102

Tsironis, L. K. (2016). Business Process Improvement through Data Mining Techniques: An Experimental Approach. In P. Papajorgji, F. Pinet, A. Guimarães, & J. Papathanasiou (Eds.), *Automated Enterprise Systems for Maximizing Business Performance* (pp. 150–169). Hershey, PA: IGI Global. doi:10.4018/978-1-4666-8841-4.ch009

Urra, O., Ilarri, S., Trillo, R., & Mena, E. (2015). Mobile Agents for a Mobile World. In V. Díaz, J. Lovelle, & B. García-Bustelo (Eds.), *Handbook of Research on Innovations in Systems and Software Engineering* (pp. 664–681). Hershey, PA: IGI Global. doi:10.4018/978-1-4666-6359-6.ch025

Vayyavur, R. (2017). Software Engineering for Technological Ecosystems. In F. Garcia-Peñalvo & A. García-Holgado (Eds.), *Open Source Solutions for Knowledge Management and Technological Ecosystems* (pp. 175–194). Hershey, PA: IGI Global. doi:10.4018/978-1-5225-0905-9.ch007

Vergidis, K. (2016). Rediscovering Business Processes: Definitions, Patterns, and Modelling Approaches. In P. Papajorgji, F. Pinet, A. Guimarães, & J. Papathanasiou (Eds.), *Automated Enterprise Systems for Maximizing Business Performance* (pp. 97–122). Hershey, PA: IGI Global. doi:10.4018/978-1-4666-8841-4.ch007

Vogelezang, F., Ramasubramani, J. K., & Arvamudhan, S. (2016). Estimation for Mobile and Cloud Environments. In A. Rosado da Cruz & S. Paiva (Eds.), *Modern Software Engineering Methodologies for Mobile and Cloud Environments* (pp. 61–87). Hershey, PA: IGI Global. doi:10.4018/978-1-4666-9916-8.ch004

Wambua, R. M., Mutua, B. M., & Raude, J. M. (2016). Stochastic Drought Forecasting Exploration for Water Resources Management in the Upper Tana River Basin, Kenya. In F. Miranda & C. Abreu (Eds.), *Handbook of Research on Computational Simulation and Modeling in Engineering* (pp. 508–539). Hershey, PA: IGI Global. doi:10.4018/978-1-4666-8823-0.ch017

Yu, L. (2016). From Android Bug Reports to Android Bug Handling Process: An Empirical Study of Open-Source Development. *International Journal of Open Source Software and Processes*, 7(4), 1–18. doi:10.4018/IJOSSP.2016100101

Index

(SNA) methods 17, 118

D

data sets 95, 118, 144
decision-making powers 58
developers 4, 6-10, 13-21, 58-60, 62-65, 67, 69, 72-76, 79, 81-82, 84, 87, 89, 91-94, 96-98, 103-107, 109, 111-114, 117, 120, 122, 130, 133-137, 141, 145

F

FOSS 1-2, 4-26, 58-60, 62, 67-69, 73, 79-80, 82, 84, 87, 89, 93-95, 98, 103-105, 109, 114, 140-148
free software 2, 4, 9, 93, 141

L

large data sets 118, 144
layered structure 58
LDAG, SPS-CELF++ 105, 107, 111

M

macro studies 58, 67

N

network analysis 17, 104-106, 111, 117-118

O

Open Source 1-2, 4, 8, 10-12, 25, 58, 67, 93, 104-105, 111, 117, 140, 146

Open Source Software 1-2, 4, 11, 58, 67, 93, 104-105, 111, 117, 140, 146
OSS 1-2, 6, 12, 16, 20, 22-26

P

personal computers 118
phenomenon 4, 6-7, 9, 18, 26, 79, 95, 104-105, 114, 140

R

real world 81, 118, 128, 140, 143, 145

S

SNA Tools 104
social network 17, 98, 104-106, 111, 117-119, 122-123, 137
Social Network Analysis 17, 104-106, 111, 117-118
software development 5, 8, 12, 18-19, 58-59, 81-82, 87, 94-95, 140, 143, 145, 147
Sourceforge.net 58-60, 63-64, 67-69, 81, 93, 95-101, 104, 117, 120

T

Top Ranked projects 67, 80-81, 83-84, 87, 92

U

utilitarian idea 141

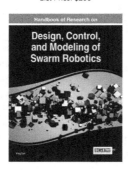

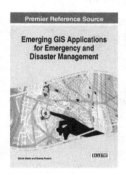
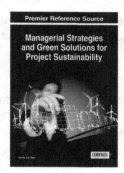